HAPPY DATA

business-led data management
for non-boring teams

Jordan Galvin

Happy Data Multimedia Publishing and Marketplace
Chicago, Illinois, USA

Happy Data
Business-Led Data Management for Non-Boring Teams

Author: Jordan Galvin

Printed in the United States.

Copyright © 2024 by Jordan Galvin

All rights reserved.

ISBN-13: 979-8-9907045-0-3
Library of Congress Control Number: 2024917810

No part of this book may be used or reproduced in any manner whatsoever without written permission of the publisher. Please purchase only authorized electronic editions, and do not participate in or encourage electronic piracy of copyrighted materials. Your support of the author's rights is appreciated.
Requests for permissions may be sent to:
hello@happydatacompany.com

About the Author

Jordan Galvin is an award-winning data and AI governance leader, lawyer, and data scientist. She is a frequent writer and speaker on business-led data management.

Jordan is also the Founder of Happy Data Multimedia Publishing and Marketplace. She named the company for her inaugural book, *Happy Data - Business-Led Data Management for Non-Boring Teams* (2024).

She currently lives in Evanston, Illinois.

Disclaimer: Unless explicitly stated otherwise, the examples, views, and policies given in this book are my own and do not necessarily reflect the positions or work product of my current or former employers. Nothing in this book constitutes legal advice, and no attorney-client relationship is created by you reading this book and completing the prompts. The advice herein is educational in nature and should not be considered a substitute for professional legal advice. References to specific software do not constitute an endorsement of that product. I have tried to make clear where I reference the work of others, but if you think I've missed a citation, please reach out to me at thehappydatabook@gmail.com.

Contents

INTRODUCTION *I Love Data* 1
CHAPTER ONE *I Dream of Data* 5
   What better place to start…: Introducing Data Management and Data Governance 6
   …than at the end? Building a Case Your Organization Will Embrace 8
      Rule #1: Make it specific. 11
      Rule #2: Make it urgent. 13
      Rule #3: Make it aspirational. 18
   Pieces of a Wheel: The Importance of Data Governance 20
   Three Choices and an Accident: Choosing an Operating Model for Your Data Department 25
   What would culture eat for breakfast during a strategy famine? Developing a Data Management Strategy 31
CHAPTER TWO *The Data Bunch* 36
   Hire #1: A Team Leader 37
      Reasons Not to Appoint a Chief Data Officer 38
      Reasons to Start at the Chief Level 40
   Hire #2: A Data Governance Leader 44
      Things to think about when hiring an internal candidate 47
      Things to think about when hiring an external candidate 48
   Who had "synergy" on their business-jargon bingo board? Identifying Other Roles to Fill 48
      Over-specializing 49
      Over-generalizing 49
      Align – Build – Connect – Deliver 50
   Creating a Guiding Coalition 51

CHAPTER THREE *Happy Data* 55

All Roads Lead to Rome—and Data Governance 56

    Principles of business-led data management 57

    Business-led data management principles in action: starting your data governance strategy 59

    Putting business-led principles to work 61

INSIGHT: Example Data Governance Guiding Principles 62

INSIGHT: Example Data Governance Short Term Goals and Roadmap 64

The Data Governance Lifecycle 67

    Phase 1: Intake 69

    Phase 2: Evaluate 69

    Phases 3-5: Plan, Pilot, and Implement 70

    Phase 6: Communicate 70

    Where to start 71

    Which data will you focus on? 72

    Drilling down to the data level 74

The 3 Ss of Data Governance 78

Phone Numbers and Fake News 79

Poor, Unfortunate Data 81

    Starting with the 3 Ss 89

    Applying the Plan, Do, Check, Act (PDCA) model 90

When to Focus on Data Quality 93

Data, and Other Intangibles: Privacy, Security, and Ethics 95

To be Let Alone: Protecting Personal Information 98

    Basics of a data privacy policy 103

To Be Secure: Data Security 104

- Creating an access program...106
- To Be Fair: Data Ethics 106
  - Hasty generalizations..107
  - Post hoc ergo propter hoc...109
  - Getting an appropriate sample size 113
  - Making sure the sample is random 113
  - Cherry picking..114
- CHAPTER FOUR *Gilligan's Data* 115
- A Camel Walks into IKEA… 116
- The Issue Management Process 118
  - Step 1: Issue Triage and Fact-finding 124
  - Step 2: Arbitration 125
  - Step 3: Appeal to Council 126
  - Step 4: Appeal to Board...127
- Model Citizen 128
  - Understanding data domains 130
  - A professional services example 131
- From Spaghetti to the Benefits of Data Virtualization.............135
- "Designed to make experts out of everyone": The Purpose of Metadata 139
  - Dewey Decimal Data: a framework for managing metadata 141
- Measuring Success 145
  - Foundations..147
  - Values 148
- 💡 INSIGHT Example Data Governance Mission Statement (part 1) 153
- 💡 INSIGHT Example Data Governance Mission Statement (part 2)

.... 153
Measures 156
Participation 161
Perception 161
Proficiency 162
Preference 163
The Quick and the Undead: Pitfalls to Avoid 163
From Big Bets to Money Pits 167
CHAPTER SIX *Data, She Wrote* 171
Go Change 172
Sustaining Engagement 175
Creating a Data Literacy Program 181
Case Study: Implementing a Literacy Program 185
CHAPTER SEVEN *The Twilight Zone* 206
For the Hitchhiker: Specific Tools for Specific Problems 209
Problem #1: Business leaders don't know how to describe what your team does 209
Problem #2: You don't have a data catalog 217
Problem #3: You can't envision how all the processes work together yet 219
Problem #4: You're being asked hard questions 222
Problem #5: You need to curtail poor data handling ethics with a policy 225
Selected Resources 238

INTRODUCTION
I Love Data

Nearly 60 percent of data management and governance programs fail to achieve their goals—and nearly a quarter achieve nothing. That's the key takeaway from the 2020 Gartner report *"The State of Data and Analytics Governance is Worse than You Think."* I don't walk far out on a limb when I say that data is at the forefront of nearly every corporate strategy. Where a data strategy may once have been a novelty, a nice-to-have, a competitive differentiator, it is now the price of admission to the modern economy. Given data's supremacy, we have to figure out what's behind all this failure.

Several tactical reasons for failed data management efforts have been put forth: a lack of key roles, technology, and funding to name a few. To be sure, a lack of resources can cripple any endeavor. But the data imperative has more attention on it than ever. Are we truly belt-tightening our way to failure? Or might there be a fundamental issue with how we frame data management and governance that undercuts its success from the start?

When I started out in the data space, two things struck me. First was data management's reputation as boring—something to "get through" on your way to something fun like analytics or data science. In reality, data management is not the traffic jam on your way to the ball game: it is the ball game.

The second thing that struck me was how much data is still treated as primarily a technical asset. True, the Body of Knowledge for data management contains activities like warehousing and architecture. And true, we use data for plenty of technical things like machine learning. But we fail when these facts persuade us that data is technical in nature.

In the real world, we constantly process data. Our eyes, ears, noses, mouths, and hands take in signals from our environment and send them to our brains to make sense of our experiences. What we observe informs how we act. We are wired to make evidence-based decisions. We are born data analysts.

In the business world, however, we hide these observations behind a firewall. We sequester them where they can't combine to form an insight. We disentangle them from business processes—both the important and the mundane—and then we struggle to piece them back together to inform enterprise priorities.

To increase the success rate of data management and governance programs, my theory is simple. Data management must be technology-enabled, but business-led. Putting the business at the center of your data management strategy sets you up to solve the problems that are front and center to your company's leadership. Once you have the support of your leadership, you are less likely to fail due to a lack of resources.

And what about that "boring" label? Is it really that important if people think data management is less exciting than building a chat bot? If you believe, as I do, that engagement drives adoption, then, yes, it is really that important. Don't let this scare you off. Being engaging doesn't mean that you're either captivatingly eloquent or irrepressibly silly. To me, an engaging program is one that is both enjoyable and purposeful.

I did not start my career in data. In fact, I went to law school because I saw the law as the conduit through which society connects goals to outcomes. Whether I ended up in practice, business, nonprofit, or government, it would be invaluable to understand how to navigate the law. However, through law school and work experience, I learned that the law doesn't diffuse through society as well as it could.

On an individual level, most low- and middle-income people do not have adequate access to the legal system. On the business side, cost of counsel has become increasingly expensive, but so have the administrative and technical burdens on law firms and legal departments. All of this creates friction in the conduit, resulting in frustrating or inadequate leverage of the law. I found that it was here that I could have the biggest impact, and that better use of data would be the most effective way to remove friction from the system.

I mention this not because it's a particularly unique or interesting story, but because it's a reminder of why data management is so important even in industries that we do not typically associate with "big data." With this in mind, you might notice a legal and professional services theme that runs through this book. While data professionals in any industry can find this book useful, I wanted to provide you with the examples and advice I wished I had more of when I first started out.

If you are new to the datasphere, consider this book your quick start guide. I will walk you through everything you need to know to get started in business-led data management. If you are a data veteran, use this book to troubleshoot specific issues, or to give you a few new ideas to try. If you are somewhere in between and starting to wonder why you were crazy enough to wade into data management, don't worry: you're among friends now.

Regardless of where you're starting, it's a big job—don't forget to have a little fun along the way.

—Jordan Galvin

CHAPTER ONE
I Dream of Data

If an ornate glass bottle appeared on my desk tomorrow, I know exactly what I would ask of the genie inside: good health, a million dollars, and useful data. Yes, I dream of data, and you may, too. Unfortunately, I am reasonably certain there's no genie coming to convince our organization's leaders to start a data program or to blink away our data quality issues. But all is not lost. In this chapter, I will help you gain leadership support for your data program the old-fashioned way. By reading this chapter and completing the prompts, you will be able to:

- ✓ Define data management
- ✓ Describe the benefits of data management in terms of business value
- ✓ Confidently pitch a data management function to organizational leadership
- ✓ Select the components of data management you will prioritize

- ✓ Select a framework that will operationalize your data management goals
- ✓ Build a strategy document that you can socialize and use regularly

What better place to start…: Introducing Data Management and Data Governance

I had just started in my first data governance role when several books introduced me to the definitions of *data management*: "the development, execution, and supervision of plans, policies, programs, and practices that deliver, control, protect, and enhance the value of data and information assets throughout their life cycles," and *data governance*[1] "the exercise of authority and control (planning, monitoring, and enforcement) over the management of data assets.[2]" I still remember my reaction:

"Wow—that's heavy."

Somewhat befuddled but not wanting to buck conventional wisdom right out of the gate, I lugged these words around like they were in an over-stuffed grocery bag—and the bottom had just split. No matter how many presentations I included them in, these definitions never got any friendlier. I was months in, and my colleagues at my firm still struggled to grasp exactly what my new team was supposed to do—or why any of it mattered. Now that I look back on those definitions, they had probably just tuned out after the second "and." Even so, the definitions weren't the problem; the problem was me.

As a data leader in my company, it is up to me to shed the image of data management as a sluggish, stilted, technical enterprise with little connection to business value. By simply parroting back over-burdened definitions to my audience, I missed the opportunity to introduce data management as an invaluable business partner. I don't mean to dramatize the effect of the definitions. Frankly, they are only emblems of the primary reason data programs fail. Often, data professionals get so wrapped up in the technical features of our mandate that we forget the business. The further we distance ourselves from the business, the greater our risk failure. Yet the training and communications on data management remain highly technical and separated components.

In this book, I am going to try something different, starting with those definitions.

Data management recognizes that data is an asset. If I asked you to think about all the things your company uses to exist and grow in market share, social leadership, and profitability, a few things would probably spring to mind: people, money, brand, knowledge, even software and equipment. In short, you would think of your organization's assets. And I am willing to bet, regardless of the business you're in, your organization invests significantly in maintaining and growing those assets. At my firm, for example, we hire top talent, and we invest in their development and well-being. We do this because people are key to our success and happy employees are a competitive advantage. Money is another classic example of an asset. Businesses work hard to control spending and maximize the amount of money they bring in because their financial position can decide the fate of their company.

Data is another of an organization's most valuable, yet unique, assets. It's not fungible or tangible, and—unlike a person or a dollar—a single point of data carries no value on its own. But, like traditional assets, if governed, data can create tremendous value. For instance, well-managed data allows businesses to:

1. Gain insight into their operations, like whether learning and development initiatives lead to increased worker productivity; whether compensation structures are

equitable; and whether they achieved an adequate return on investment from software purchases;

2. Provide better products and services by tailoring recommendations to specific customer interests or reinforcing traditional services with data analysis;

3. Grow the business by providing data as a service or by assessing where there is growth potential for customers, products, or geographies; and

4. Participate in the next wave of "killer" technology, like Generative Artificial Intelligence (AI).

Data allows us to do all of these things and more, but only if it accessible, reliable, and secure. And that is the goal of data management: to govern data as we would our other assets so that we can use it to advance the overall strategy of the business.

…than at the end? Building a Case Your Organization Will Embrace

The phrase "drinking from a fire hose" barely captures what it feels like when unending demands for data surround you. Data is a piece of, if not the foundation for, all corporate initiatives. Indeed, with the explosion of AI, the fact of data's importance is clearer now than even last year. Enchanted by the possibilities, your organization's eyes are sure to be bigger than its stomach. The trick is to encourage that enthusiasm while remaining clear-eyed and candid about the hard work that lies ahead.

If we're honest with ourselves, the first people needing reality checks were probably those naive optimists in the mirror. Who among us hasn't been drawn to the promise of better business outcomes using those silver bullets called "data science" and "digital transformation"? But at some point, we realize that making good on those promises requires more than a brilliant thought; it requires a strong technical foundation and an even stronger business tie. Like the old starry-eyed, genie-scouting you, your organization's leaders may want a team to implement data science, analytics, and AI from day one. But you know better.

It's now up to you to help your company's leaders know what you know. Luckily, you can do this without giving up on that end goal of data science and AI. Instead, you can gain buy-in for your ideal data team by recognizing your company's ultimate goals for its data and then showing why your proposal is the best way to reach those goals. It's not that you want to begin at the end, but rather that you want to "begin," as highly effective people do, "with the end in mind.[3]"

We begin with the end in mind first and foremost when we understand that the best intentions don't guarantee success. This is made clear in a 2020 Gartner survey showing that data governance and data management programs often fail to achieve their stated objectives.[4] While three-quarters of respondents said they had a goal of optimizing data and reducing costs, only 45 percent felt they had been successful. Nearly two-thirds of respondents began a data governance program to mitigate regulatory, financial, and ethical risks; only 44 percent reported success. Seventy-six percent hoped to use data as a competitive advantage and generate revenue, but a pitiful 27 percent realized this goal. Finally, nearly a fourth of respondents felt their programs had achieved nothing. Is success with data a coin toss, then? Check out Figure 1 to see what those same survey respondents attributed their failure to.

I Dream of Data

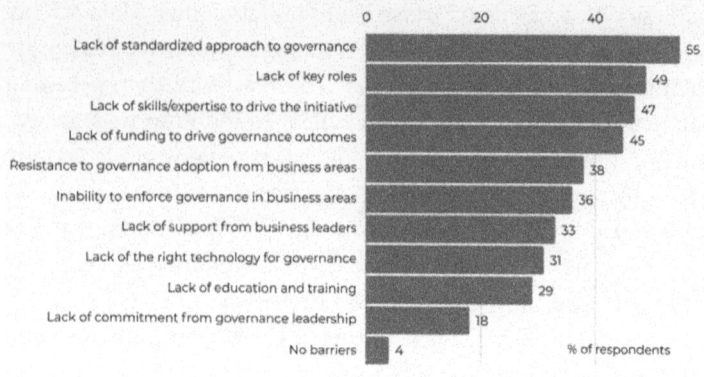

Figure 1

The volume of barriers identified in Figure 1 alone might make you feel like you're up a creek. But I see a silver-lining here: while this survey pulled out "Lack of support from business leadership" as an independent choice, most of the survey's remaining barriers exist either directly or indirectly because of insufficient executive support. That is, if you have executive support, you are more likely to get the key roles, funding, support for governance and more that you need to be successful.

The primacy of executive support here makes sense. A company's executives are responsible for not just providing resources, but also for blocking and tackling when chaos swarms. Conversely, they also have the power to shut things down—either purposely or through neglect. So, to ensure we don't go the way of our counterparts in the Gartner survey, we must win the support of senior leadership. But be careful not to mistake enthusiasm with support. That means, yes, enticing them with a vision for the future, but also ensuring they understand that excellence will be hard-won. From the first conversations, we can garner informed support for our work by making sure our leaders understand the importance of data management to the business, and the risk of a slip-shod effort—or of no effort at all. This can make pitching a new data function feel like an overwhelming task, but it's a manageable one if you scrap the giant definitions and follow these three rules instead.

Rule #1: Make it specific.

I have bought a lot of products and services in my day. Sure, I've had my impulse buys, but I don't recall ever being persuaded into a big investment based on the idea that I might need something someday for some problem that I can't quite explain yet but that other people are talking a lot about.

Starting a data program is not an impulse buy: it's an investment. Any financial, human, and political capital leaders spend on your program are resources they are not investing elsewhere. Why are you a good bet?

Being sufficiently specific doesn't mean you need to have all problems identified and solved on day one. You will uncover problems along the way, either naturally or by design. Rapid technology advances also mean you will need to leave space for some experimentation. But you risk adding to the uncertainty around data and AI if you go to early meetings with your senior leaders and ask them to provide you with resources to figure out what the company's problems are. Remember: you already have an idea of why you need a data program. What made you come to that realization? Now is the time to supplement your initial, formative ideas with even more research.

Here are some questions you may want to consider in your research (trust me, your senior leaders will likely have the same questions):

1. What are data governance and data management? Why does the research say they are important?

2. How are your peer and aspirational organizations using data

governance and management? What have been the outcomes?

3. What specific data is important to your organization? Do you process a lot of sensitive data? Do you have a lot of sales data, like SKUs and transaction details? Think about who the organization's clients or customers are. Think about the services the organization offers. Then think about how any organization runs its business. You will surely find human resources, marketing, and finance data that is ripe for improvement.

4. What evidence do you have that important data could be better managed? Do you see data that is inaccurate, untimely, incomplete, or inconsistent? What projects have fallen short because of inadequate or low-quality data? Do you see a lot of code created to deal with exceptions or to transform data into a usable state? Are copies of data lying around outside the source system? Amass both a qualitative and quantitative pile of evidence.

5. What challenges or advantages do you foresee based on your knowledge of the organization's culture or structure? For example, if your company's structure is flat, you will have to gain buy-in from each individual person, rather than rely on directors and managers to spread the word to those under them.

6. So far, you have visualized the end state and you have discovered where you are currently. You should now be ready to tell the organization what it needs to do now and what it needs to do next. What order of operations will you suggest?

7. Finally, what can you learn about your leaders that will allow you to speak in a way they will hear you? How open are they to change? How can each be persuaded? Are some more persuaded by data? By testimonials?

The ease of answering these questions will depend in part on whether you are pitching from inside the organization, or whether the company has recognized the need and is now hiring for your role. In the former scenario, you will likely have a head start because you already know basics about the company, like its culture and clientele. In the latter, experience can tell you where the most likely traps and gaps are. But you will need to spend more time in this discovery phase to understand the company's eccentricities as well as someone pitching from within. Regardless, you can use the above questions as a guide at any stage to ensure you are delivering on-target advice.

Rule #2: Make it urgent.

Certain circumstances almost always raise the "urgency" flag: risk of significant monetary or reputational harm (as in the case of a data breach); sudden need for agility (as in the case of a pandemic or a dying technology product); and losing (or fear of losing) ground amongst competitors in a rapidly changing industry (as in the case of technological breakthroughs). In some instances, the "urgency factors" will write themselves. If you know your company is going to become subject to a new data privacy law carrying hefty financial penalties, you will have little trouble convincing your organization's leaders to act. Usually, though, you will need to draw out the urgency for them. Consider the following scenarios.

Protecting your organization from data breaches

Since the dawn of computers, bad actors have tried to gain

access to digital information. No company is safe from potential attacks. Indeed, fewer information security professionals are fired after a breach than in years past because we'd soon run out of people to fill these roles. Nonetheless, data breaches can still result in significant monetary and reputational harm—especially when it reveals a company's subpar data handling practices.

If you were an adult living in the United States in the last decade, you probably had your personal data compromised in the 2017 Equifax data breach. You are unlikely to have forgotten the "dumpster fire[5]" response to the theft of nearly 60 percent of American adults' addresses, social security numbers, and dates of birth. But let's relive it for a moment. Equifax is one of the three main credit reporting agencies (CRAs) in the United States. CRAs collect your personal and financial information from businesses, banks, landlords, and others to create and share a composite profile of your creditworthiness to your would-be lenders. In March of 2017, the Department of Homeland Security alerted the three main CRAs—Equifax included—of a software vulnerability and available patch. Equifax did not apply the patch until late July 2017, after it had already discovered suspicious activity. It then took Equifax more than a month to notify consumers of the breach, costing valuable time to mitigate damage.

We now know that Equifax's failure to promptly patch a known vulnerability allowed members of the Chinese military to spend nearly three months looting American, British, and Canadian citizens' most sensitive data.[6] The fallout was dramatic. In the week following news of the breach, Equifax's stock plummeted 35 percent[7]—erasing nearly $6 billion of market value. In 2019, the breach cost Equifax an additional half billion dollars in settlement[8] with the US Government, and I personally received my $17 settlement check in 2023 (yes, I filled out the form—worth it).

Many of us may also recall the Marriott data debacle of 2018. In a catastrophic failure to properly integrate data following the acquisition of Starwoods Hotels, Marriott spilled the sensitive data of over 500 million people.[9] They managed the aftermath of the breach much more competently than Equifax (though the bar could hardly have been lower), and thus were spared the type of financial harm of Equifax's scale. However, the number of reservations at Marriott hotels continued to slide a year after the breach, and as late as 2023 the hotel chain's legal and reputational hardship continued.[10]

Equifax and Marriot are both giant brands, with deep pockets and long histories. If this is how breaches rocked those companies, a breach could be the death knell for a start-up or younger company. In a 2020 survey, two-thirds of respondents predictably reported that they "trust[ed] a company less" after a data breach, while a quarter said the breach caused them to stop doing business with the company altogether.[11] Unlike Equifax, which is a mandatory reporting agency, most companies exist because of the ongoing goodwill of their customers. Protect their data; protect your company.

Addressing data privacy regulations

Even absent a major event like the Equifax and Marriot breaches, organizations face an increasingly regulated data environment affecting their daily operations. We will discuss these regulations in more detail in Chapter 3. But when you are drawing out the urgency for your leadership in your early conversations, it suffices to outline the universe of laws out there. This could include laws protecting data in certain sectors, like health or financial data. But the sectoral laws have been around for a while, so your company is likely familiar enough with their mandates. It may be most practical at this stage to highlight those general data protection laws that may be newer for your company. The General Data Protection Regulation (GDPR) in Europe is among the most familiar, but the latest UN Trade & Development[12] data shows 137 out of 194 countries around the globe have adopted data privacy legislation. Should you raise the specter of complying with one of these emerging laws, you will surely find heads begin to nod in understanding.

Your organization no doubt (I hope) has professionals already dedicated to cyber- and information security, and perhaps even a data privacy counsel to handle the legal aspects. But lest your audience think that will be enough to adequately protect sensitive data, have them consider this: who will implement the security rules on the databases? Who will classify each and every data set as sensitive or not? Who will respond to the requests to access or delete records? Data management professionals are vital members of the data privacy and security team—in practice if not by title.

Though incredibly important, the leaders of your organization will probably not need a lot of convincing to prioritize data privacy. My advice here would be to make this a pillar of your pitch, but focus mainly on how you would collaborate with the existing professionals in your organization to optimize your data privacy program. Of course, tailor this to the reality of the situation you are in: if more time needs to be spent here because you sense the current protections lacking, prepare to make that case.

Promoting business agility

Urgency doesn't end with the threat of potential legal action. I think you'd be hard-pressed to find an organization that didn't find itself needing to adjust its operations almost overnight at the breakout of the COVID-19 pandemic. When "2020 became 2025, [13] " organizations who had previously digitized their operations were able to quickly shift to remote work with little interruption. Those organizations that did not found themselves needing to pivot—and fast.

While the pandemic is an extreme example of sudden business agility, organizations constantly evolve to meet new challenges or capture new opportunities. Like a sudden pivot, these more commonplace progressions can either be helped or hindered by the company's data practices. Suppose your company is looking to merge with or acquire another company. We are so familiar with the press and customer experience surrounding these combinatorial companies that it's easy to underestimate the effort it takes to merge the two organizations' data. But consider for a moment the torment of a young couple moving in together for the first time. They beam as they tell their family and all their friends that their relationship is so strong that they're ready to join lives. He decided to move into her house to live closer to all the good restaurants; if she's being honest, having him contribute to half the mortgage isn't a bad thing.

What she doesn't realize until he shows up with his first box is that—oh no—he's bringing all his stuff. "Where amongst my French countryside decor," she wonders, "did he envision his samurai swords going? And he brought his toaster? And his coffee maker? But I already have both those things." Like these two poor souls, two merging companies are just as likely to couple, only for their collective hearts to sink when the data from one company just doesn't go with the data from the other.

Subsuming someone else's data without a clear governance structure in place is possible. But aside from creating annoying decorative mismatches, it's also expensive, time-consuming, risky (as we learned from the Marriott example) and will keep good portions of your IT team underwater for the foreseeable future. Knowing this, if you are in a smaller or younger company, think about how the state of your data might make your company a more or less attractive target for acquisition. The same holds true for any method of expanding the business—whether we grow into new geographies, product lines, or markets. The strength of your data management practices will determine the ease with which you can expand into novel areas.

Embracing the potential of AI

Finally, generate a sense of urgency for your audience by reminding them of what every good business person has a healthy dose of: FOMO. Yes, fear of missing out. We should all be afraid of missing out on the AI revolution. History is littered with extinct businesses that failed to keep up with the times. At the dawn of this "Fourth Industrial Revolution," many worry that AI will replace their jobs. The dangers to businesses who don't have the foundation upon which to build and use AI products get less media attention. Data-immature businesses risk a range of consequences, from failing to realize efficiency gains, to losing ground to more agile competitors, to being able innovate the core business model when it's clear change is the only choice. Surely your company is already planning for a future with AI. But do they know that data is the foundation?

Researchers from Cambridge, New York University, and University College London lay out why data governance paves the way for successful AI governance.[14] First, they point out, AI is only one part of a full data lifecycle that includes data collection, storage, use, and disposal. AI is constructed using the outputs of the data governance lifecycle. Given this, whatever level of data quality and interoperability you ensure in the data governance lifecycle is the level of quality and interoperability you can expect in your AI. Data governance does more than help prepare the organization technically for AI: it ensures compliant data handling practices, and it coordinates stakeholder engagement. The list could go on, but the message to convey to your leadership is simple: data governance must lay the foundation for AI. If your company has not implemented data governance, they must—or they will be left behind.

Rule #3: Make it aspirational.

Think back on the moments that spurred you to act. What

emotion did you feel? My guess is that you felt one of two things: fear or inspiration. Rule #2 deals with the emotion of fear, but I would caution against relying on fear alone to move your audience.

First, fear can be managed—in a sense, it is bounded by its cause. Neutralize the cause of the fear, and you're spurred to act no longer. Whether rightly or wrongly, the leaders in your organization may assuage their fears by hiring data privacy and security professionals and failing to see how additional data management adds value.

On the other hand, what people will do when they are inspired is nearly boundless. We've built products, started companies, formed governments, and painted masterpieces. These are hard, inconvenient exercises that we can't help but try because we're enamored with what could be. Rule #2 is largely focused on helping your organization control risk. Rule #3 is about helping it capture opportunity.

Humans thrive off inspiration. But as *Rule #3: Make it Aspirational* suggests, inspiration will get you going, but it won't keep you going. Getting people to undertake a longer-term commitment to not just do something, but become something—getting them to aspire to something—is where true transformation happens. Think of giving inspiration to your audience as your foot in the door. To give them aspiration is to show them meaningful, exciting, and achievable changes they can make to become the type of organization they want.

What does your organization want to be? What does it say it wants to be to its clients? What does it want to be able to do better than anyone else? Because data is an asset, it can be used to further whatever strategic goals your company has for itself. But the line from input to outcome may not be as clear to executives who are used to working with traditional assets. When you are pitching a data management program to your leadership, close this logical gap for them. Show them you know the business's aspirations, and illustrate how you will use data to supplement other assets in pursuit of those goals. (If you're not totally sure what the concrete steps are yet, then you are in the right place. The rest of this book helps you develop steps that speak to the unique position of your company.)

Following the advice and suggestions outlined in the preceding sections of this chapter, you now have a plan for your opening pitch: you're going to be specific about the challenges, you're going to get them to feel the risk of inaction, and you are going to create a vision of the future they can't wait to build. Now's not the time to leave them hanging. Now is your chance to show that you have the solution they need. The next section explains how to build your data management program.

Pieces of a Wheel: The Importance of Data Governance

Data management is all about controlling risk and capturing opportunity, so each component of your data program should serve one or both of these goals. The DAMA International Data Management Body of Knowledge (DAMA-DMBOK) frames data management as a wheel of eleven disciplines (Figure 2), with data governance forming the center and structure of the wheel (and thus supporting each of the other ten disciplines).[15]

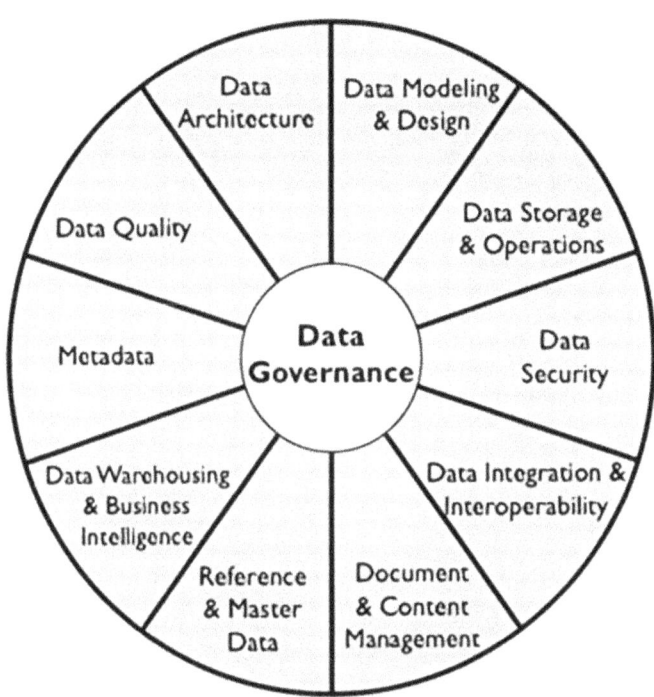

Copyright© 2017 DAMA International

Figure 2

Effective data management does not necessitate that each slice of the wheel is performed at the same scale. Which of these components (described in "Quick Reference: Data Management Disciplines, Briefly") to incorporate into your data operations will depend on the demands of the organization and whether any are addressed by an existing department. Especially as a nascent team, you'll want to focus on building a foundation that addresses the immediate needs of the business and propels you to higher levels of maturity.

QUICK
REFERENCE:

Data Management Disciplines, Briefly

1. **Data Governance**—defines and maintains stewards and standards for data assets and guides all other data management functions.

2. **Data Architecture**—describes and designs systems used for storing, transforming, and moving data.

3. **Data Modeling & Design**—represents data requirements via conceptual, semantic, logical, or physical relationship models.

4. **Data Storage & Operations**—designs, implements, and supports systems that store data.

5. **Data Security**—ensures appropriate access in alignment with data security policies and best practices.

6. **Data Integration & Interoperability**—moves and consolidates data between and within systems.

7. **Document & Content Management**—manages the lifecycle of data and information.

8. **Reference & Master Data**—manages the availability and quality of critical and shared data.

9. **Data Warehousing & Business Intelligence**—supports

reporting, query, and analysis.

10. **Metadata Management**—ensures availability, quality, and usability of metadata.

11. **Data Quality Management**—ensures data is sufficient and fit for consumption.

SOURCE: *DAMA-DMBOK*

Let's say, for example, that your company has just become subject to new data privacy regulations and must enact a system to handle personal information and data subject requests. Although your organization has other, long-term aspirations for its data, these privacy regulations pose an immediate risk. Comparing your organizational landscape to the DAMA wheel, you note that the business already has an information security function (possibly covering the data security spoke of the wheel) and a records team who focus on document and content management. These two groups should be your partners in the data privacy effort. To ensure compliance with the privacy regulations, the data you control must be accurate and available—hallmarks of data quality. You will likely also need to define standards and policies regarding access, storage, and use of this private data, so you will need a strong data governance arm.

Other segments of the wheel, like data warehousing & business intelligence and data modeling & design are prerequisites for analytics and other advanced technical functions. In this hypothetical, you could probably focus on these pieces once you have established the domains that have a direct impact on data privacy management: data security, data quality, document & content management, and data governance.

In truth, even if your organization's data problems are

more systemic than acute, data governance is always a great place to start. Some organizations may never even touch the other parts of the wheel, and indeed others may contain their efforts to governance and quality of a subset of data. Thinking again of our data privacy example, that business may want to focus all of its energy on controlling accuracy, access, and auditability of personally identifiable information.

Many large companies may also want to incorporate metadata management and data storage and integration into their initial strategy. Connecting myriad systems to each other (resulting in what is often referred to as a "spaghetti architecture" because when diagrammed it looks like a bowl of spaghetti), rather than via a centralized hub, results in higher costs and greater risk. Logically, we know it is easier and less expensive to implement security and privacy rules on one system than on twenty. Further, proliferation of systems which do similar things results in increased cost, duplication of effort, and silos that develop unique data dialects. The DAMA wheel is therefore like a suit before it's been tailored. Pieces can be added, subtracted, stretched, and folded to fit the requirements, size, and aspirations of the business.

One thing is for certain, though: data governance is the center of the wheel for a reason. Without strong data governance, undertaking any other piece of the wheel will be minimally effective, regardless of how talented the people are or how great the technology is. As the center of the wheel, data governance also serves as the centerpiece of this book. This book is, after all, meant to set you up with the best foundation possible. We touched on governance briefly here, but you can read much more in Chapter 3.

Three Choices and an Accident: Choosing an Operating Model for Your Data Department

An operating framework is a critical piece of infrastructure that guides data management to a path of value and accelerates buy-in and commitment from all stakeholders. When building a data team, one of the first things to construct is your department's operating framework.

To build an operating framework is, in essence, to build a system of government for your organization's data. Typically overseen by a data governance function, an operating model consists of the roles and processes that shepherd data from current-state to governed-state. Your operating model will define how the company makes policy decisions, how it resolves issues, who is accountable for each piece or set of data, and how the data community will interact. Regardless of how wide or narrow your focus is, effective data governance is, at its core, about people and value.

Most data governance literature describes three types of operating frameworks: centralized, decentralized (sometimes called "replicated"[16]), and federated.

The Centralized Approach

The centralized approach (Figure 3) consists of a single governing body that oversees all activities in all domains. Perhaps unsurprisingly, this is considered the most formal and mature operating model. With an executive (or other senior level) position overseeing and coordinating data management, the organization enjoys a clear chain of accountability and more efficient decision-making.

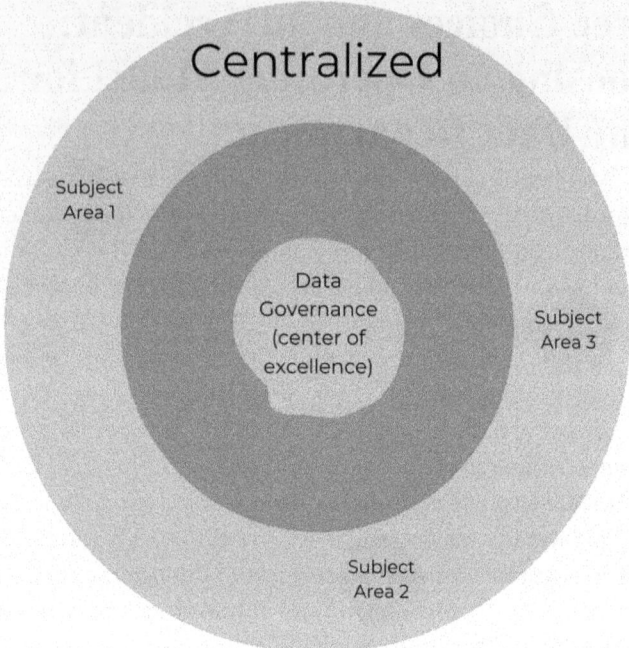

Figure 3

However, the source of a centralized structure's benefits can also present disadvantages. For example, building a completely new structure that depends on the compliance of those not within your direct control requires a significant amount of change management. Additionally, those on the central data team will most likely have less knowledge of the governed subject areas than the professionals working in those areas. It is thus incumbent on the members of the data team to learn enough about the business areas to make appropriate decisions and recommendations. For these reasons, though a centralized model denotes maturity it is not necessarily ideal for every company.

A centralized approach works best in environments with one or more of the following characteristics:

- The organization is small (of course, "small" is relative, but if your company is sitting at 1,000 or fewer employees, you could be small enough for a centralized approach)
- The organization has one or two distinct, primary lines of business and/or operating regions
- The organization is ready, logistically and culturally, to create this new structure

None of these are hard and fast rules, to be sure. But when you consider an organization with characteristics opposite to those above, you can see (1) how much effort if would take for the central data team to maintain effective ties to each unit, and (2) how much further removed the central team would be from where day-to-day decisions are made. Essentially, what you would gain in structural simplicity you would lose in agility and potential effectiveness.

The Decentralized (or Replicated) Approach

On the opposite end of the spectrum, a decentralized model exists when an organization replicates the same governing apparatus and standards within each of its business units. The hallmark of this type of structure is its lack of a central leader. A decentralized operating model may have regional or departmental governance leaders, as shown in Figure 4. But, some decentralized teams may have even less leadership than this — perhaps one or two governance analysts or stewards who look after a particular type of data.

In contrast with the centralized model, a decentralized approach can be implemented and altered relatively quickly. The decentralized governance professionals are also, by definition, a lot closer to the work of the business units. This means that the governance work and the business work could become self-reinforcing. The downside of a decentralized approach is that it becomes extremely challenging—if not impossible—to reach enterprise-wide consensus.

A decentralized structure may work in very large companies with little overlap between departments or product lines. Probably only a small percentage of organizations would fit this bill. Think of, for example, a company like Meta. They might choose to have distinct data management and governance teams at each business unit (Facebook, Instagram, WhatsApp) and at the parent company itself. Where you're in a "company of companies," decentralization could be a fine choice.

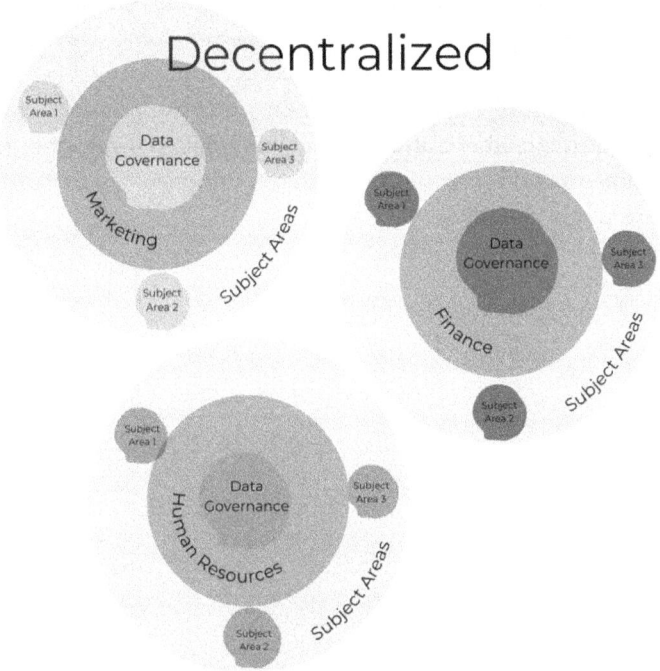

Figure 4

The Federated Approach

The federated model features a central governing body that coordinates data management efforts across various business units. Figure 5 shows how the data strategy is centralized in a Center of Excellence, while execution is distributed among the several units and subject areas. The overlap between the circles representing subject areas in the diagram depicts how a federated model allows for regional or departmental priorities—and even regional governance of certain data—while maintaining enterprise standards. A federated operating model thus allows for consistent rules and procedures while encouraging collaboration among business units.

The main drawback to this approach is its complexity. You must expend energy understanding whether some data is truly regional or whether it must be governed at the enterprise level; you will likely have some departments that are more willing to collaborate than others; and you may find that your priorities (i.e., the organization's priorities) are misaligned with certain department's priorities.

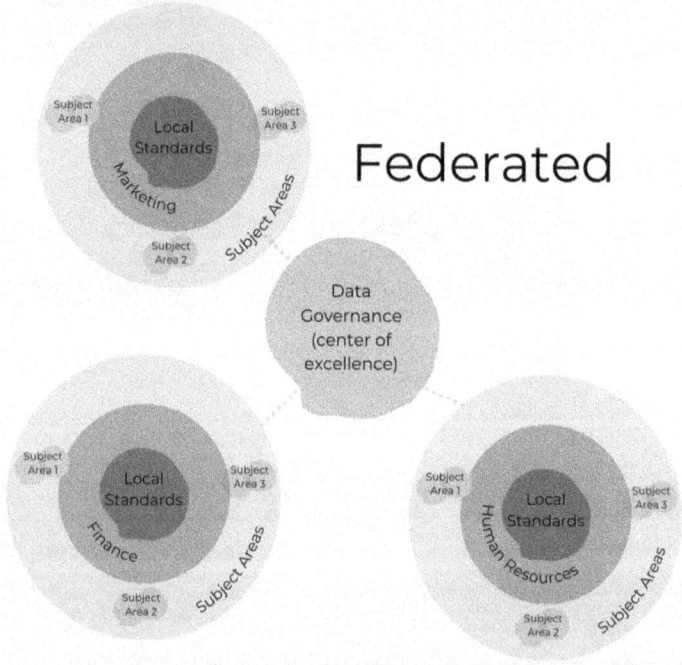

Figure 5

The Accidental Approach

Of course, these are just the operating frameworks that would exist as a result of some choice or design. In all likelihood, your organization currently exists in a state of accidental, ad hoc governance. In an ad hoc situation, we're all really just trying to get by. We implement data structures and customs based on what makes sense at the time, and coordination between—or even among—teams is sparse if it exists at all.

There is no one, best way to structure a data program. Rather, your choice of operating model should consider both the structure and culture of your organization, as well as the pieces of the data management wheel you chose to focus on.

What would culture eat for breakfast during a strategy famine? Developing a Data Management Strategy

My son is a gamer. He's only 7, but he kicks my tail at every game we play. When he was learning to play chess two summers ago, we'd encourage him to pause before making a move. We'd ask, "look at the board. What's your strategy?" I don't know how long it took for him to begin doing this naturally, but somewhere along the line he started solving all problems this way. When he's doing his math homework, he will read the problem out loud and then say, "my strategy is to…." When he wants to learn a new soccer skill: "my strategy is to…." What if he had ended these sentences with "be good at math," and "be better than my competition"? Would he have solved his math problem or learned his soccer skill? Certainly not with the help of those strategies.

Being "data-driven" is not a strategy. Buying technology is not a strategy. Just like "being good at games" is not the strategy my son uses when he beats me at tic-tac-toe for the 10th time in a row. Remember the aspirations we talked about previously? Your strategy buttresses those aspirations with concrete steps for how you will get there. Your strategy is where you will survey the game board, acknowledge the moves that have already been played, and craft your next moves based on that environment.

If you've been following along, you have thus far determined the broad themes you intend to address with your data management practice (refer to the earlier section "…than at the end? Building a Case Your Organization Will Embrace"). You have even sketched a proposed operating model (see the section "Three Choices and an Accident: Choosing an Operating Model for Your Data Department"). Temptation may now try to suck you straight into implementation-mode. But I would caution you to first pause and zoom out.

Before putting pen to paper on your strategy, you will also want to understand your internal environment—that is, your organization and your position within it. Below are some of the questions you will want to consider.

1. How is your organization structured? What are its various business units? How does it make its money?

2. Who are your organization's customers?

3. Is the organization ready to collaborate, or are departmental silos a major problem?

4. Where will the data function sit? How does the rest of the organization typically interact with the group housing the data function?

5. Will gaining and keeping executive support be a challenge? Is the organization prepared to devote resources to data management?

Honestly answer these questions so that you can set big goals and high standards while not over-promising or setting your team up for failure. From this foundation, you are ready to draft an initial strategy.

Components of a Good Data Strategy

The components of a good data strategy are not dissimilar to those of other business strategies you may have seen or written in the past. However, especially where you are proposing a new concept, you may want to provide more detail on each component than you would normally. So often, strategy documents become untouched artifacts instead of the handy compasses we need. But this does not have to be the case if you spend considerable time strategizing with your relevant stakeholders. Consider including the strategy components in the table below:

Component	Consider
Introduction	What time period will this strategy cover? Who owns this strategy? Who needs to sign off on it?
Guiding Principles	What are your team's mission and vision? What are the key themes on which you aim to build your team and strategy?
Long-term Directional Goals	Similar to, but more detailed than, your mission and vision, what are 4-6 "state of being" goals you want to achieve in the long term? In other words, what are some things you want to be able to assert 2-5 years from now? For example, "Our critical and priority data is trustworthy and fit for its intended use."
Roles and	What types of roles will comprise your

Responsibilities	core team? What ancillary groups (e.g., steering or oversight) must be created? How should these groups be structured? What activities will each role or group be responsible for? Have groups been vested with the proper authority to make decisions?
Main Program Components and Initiatives	What tools, activities, or systems will you build, implement, or sponsor to achieve your short- and long-term goals?
Measures of Program Success	How will you determine the health of your program? How will you determine the health of your projects? How will you measure progress toward your goals?
Potential Barriers to Success	Based on research and experience, what do you foresee as threats to achieving your stated goals?
Short-term Goals and Road Map	Have you benchmarked yourself against a maturity model? If so, what level of maturity are you at now, and where do you want to be by the end of the strategy period? What specific activities will you schedule to ensure you reach the next level of maturity? Have you vetted your schedule with stakeholders to confirm practicability?

| *Appendices* | Include exhibits, diagrams, worked examples, or other clarifying materials. |

Table 1

Don't worry if you don't know the answers to all of these questions right now. Going through the remainder of this book will help you draft the components of a strategy that is uniquely suited to your organization's potential. Getting the strategy document right takes a lot of effort. I, myself, spent several weeks crafting a data governance strategy that only looked two years into the future. But now, hardly a week goes by that I don't call on my strategy for presentations, project guidance, schedule checks, and benchmarking. You can see snippets of my data governance strategy in Chapter 3: Happy Data.

CHAPTER TWO
The Data Bunch

I work with an amazing team. If I had to build a team from the ground up, these are the exact people I would pick. (Of course, a few of them I did pick, but I'd pick them again if I could.) I've tried to identify key characteristics they each possess so that I might pass on a nugget of advice on how to pick winners, but ultimately, I think it boils down to this: good people are drawn to good people; talented people are drawn to good work. To draw in and retain talent, number one: be someone you'd want to work for. Number two, have a solid vision for the team and for the role that you're hiring. No one wants to start a job feeling unsure of the assignment or that their position is precarious. Neither of these pieces of advice are revolutionary. But my third piece of advice might surprise you. Because data as a discipline is a business-technical hybrid, the perfect candidates might come from unexpected places.

On my team, few of us have degrees in, or started our

careers in, the field we now master. We have software engineers who studied English, data engineers who studied Business, and lawyers who now analyze data. On paper these may have been weaknesses, but I think it's our superpower. Our diversity of experience, as a group and on the person level, allows us to solve problems more creatively, communicate more effectively to diverse audiences, and empathize better with our customers. We are also a highly motivated team. We are all on this team out of a genuine curiosity and love of the field. So, while technical skills are table-stakes for certain roles, the makeup of the team should reflect your understanding of data as a business asset first and a technical asset second.

By reading this chapter and completing the prompts, you will be able to:

- ✓ Consider whether to hire a chief data officer first
- ✓ Weigh the pros and cons of hiring internal and external candidates
- ✓ Describe key roles
- ✓ Understand the importance of a carefully crafted guiding coalition

---

Hire #1: A Team Leader

So, who should your first hires be? You will need a team leader, and you will need someone to focus on data governance. Depending on your needs, these may be one and the same.

Hail to the...Director?

While I encourage organizations or ambitious individuals within them to start managing data at whatever altitude they can, the level of impact and success will be directly proportional to the amount of support given from the top. That means that, yes, you will need support at the chief level. But does that mean you must begin your journey with a chief data officer? Not at all. In fact, if managing data as an asset is a completely new discipline for your organization, growing your nascent team from within an existing department could grease the wheels for larger scale transformation.

Reasons Not to Appoint a Chief Data Officer

Why might hiring a chief data officer first be against your company's best interest? Two main reasons.

Battle for Legitimacy

While there is a lot to be said for grass-roots efforts' success in creating sustainable culture shifts, that's not the only reason your company may want to put off hiring a chief data officer. An implicit bias awaits nearly every new chief—a phenomenon I call the New "X" Paradox. We've come to expect certain "CxO" positions in most organizations: CEOs, CFOs, and CIOs to name a few. But if you've noticed some creative new titles popping up in the C-suite, you're not alone. Check out some of the most intriguing:[17]

- Chief Budget Officer
- Chief Happiness Officer
- Chief User Experience Officer
- Chief Storytelling Officer
- Chief Customer Officer
- Chief Freelance Relationship Officer
- Chief Inclusion Officer
- Chief Sustainability Officer
- Chief Growth Officer
- Chief Automation Officer

- Chief Behavioral Officer
- Chief Party Officer
- Chief Learning Officer
- Chief Innovation Officer
- Chief Data Officer

Value-based judgments aside, each of these new Xs faces a battle for legitimacy. And therein lies the paradox: the organization must have seen the benefit in creating and hiring for this role, yet these new chiefs must constantly prove their worth. They may often find their voice carries less weight on important topics than their counterparts', they may have a smaller budget and team, and they may find existing departments hesitant to hand over work that once belonged to them.

Several causes might explain this phenomenon. For example, people can smell a PR-play a mile away; perhaps they think you're just a fad they need to wait out. Or maybe they're threatened. Maybe they've done a lot of work in this area and now you're here to take it away. Maybe somebody high up saw the value in this role, but others still need some convincing. Maybe others in the organization interviewed for that role but you got it instead and now, well, how you're doing things is fine but it's not how they would have done it.

You get the point. Now, would-be chief data officers won't likely have the same fight as those with other, eye-roll-inducing gimmicky titles ("Dream Alchemist[18]" anyone?), but the other challenges will remain.

Creating a New Silo
Second, by starting your data efforts with a chief data officer, you could end up creating a new silo instead of dismantling existing ones. Again, this is true for any chief. Any time an organization sets up a new vertical, it risks detaching it

from the rest of the business. With or without the presence of a chief data officer, the data team must make a conscious effort to integrate itself and show that it can enhance every other team in the company. A highly collaborative chief data officer can ease this transition; an isolationist chief can sour the company on data indefinitely.

Reasons to Start at the Chief Level

Of course, the flip side of this is that it may be in your best interest to start at the chief level. If you are in a technically mature organization—one where the value of data is culturally inherent—hiring a chief data officer first could be a great way to energize the organization and ensure it has a strong leader at the helm as it ventures into the world of advanced data architectures, compliance, or artificial intelligence. Separating the function from IT could, both in name and practice, keep the data team from becoming overly technical at the expense of the business. Whether your organization is ready for a chief data officer—and thus whether you can successfully navigate the New "X" Paradox— depends largely on how readily the company leaders and employees accept your value proposition, not just in name, but in substance.

Building an Environment That Supports Success

The optimal first team leader will therefore depend on the organization. And, in truth, many of you reading this are in a role where this decision has already been made for you. The good news in that case is that regardless of which route was chosen, a leader at any level can succeed as long as they are in an environment with certain elements. A fruitful environment for a data leader is one in which they are surrounded by an organization with clout; where they have the authority to make decisions; and where they have access to resources. The following sections take each of these requirements in turn.

First, the team leader **must be surrounded by a department with clout**. A time (or two, or three) will come where the luster of your vision has faded, where unpopular but necessary actions must be taken, and where the priorities of other departments deliver you less charitable partners. In these situations, you will need some muscle to keep things moving.

I had the opportunity once to hear Robert Cialdini speak about his famous six principles of influence.[19] If you aren't familiar with Cialdini's research, the basic idea is that people are predisposed to be persuaded by six primary types of intrinsic philosophies:

1. **Reciprocity**—our innate aversion to being indebted to another person;

2. **Commitment and Consistency**—our desire to remain consistent with our prior acts or positions;

3. **Social Proof**—because when your mom used to ask, "if everyone jumped off a bridge, would you do it too?" the answer was, apparently, "yes";

4. **Liking**—if we like someone, we are more likely to agree with them;

5. **Authority**—if someone is more knowledgeable or experienced, we are more likely to agree with them; and

6. **Scarcity**—because we always want what we can't have.

Not to quibble with Cialdini, but it's really hard to

consistently pull these levers. Often, we just don't have the time, the energy, or the skill to win over some of the tougher cases. Plus, each of these six factors are implicitly based on perception. I may, in fact, be more knowledgeable on a subject than you, but if you don't perceive me as being more knowledgeable, I've either got to convince you that I am, or I've got to pick another method from the list.

Likewise, there's a reason we were never really convinced by our mom's "bridge" logic: because it was a straw man argument and we knew it. This underpins a fragility with the social proof lever. Like authority, it relies on someone's perceptions of how similar they are to the group we're comparing them to (and how similar their two situations are). All of this is not to say that each of these six principles can't be effective. Of course they can. But sometimes, persuasion yields to practicality. Sometimes you just need enforcement power to drive compliance, clear a path, or create accountability. Can your data team access someone with this power?

Second, the team leader **must have the authority to make decisions.** When I was learning to ride a horse, my legs and voice weren't strong enough to persuade my stubborn, 1200-pound steed to do anything requiring forward momentum. Week after week, my instructor would lead the horse—and me on top—around the arena before letting me take the reins. She'd remove the lead rope from the horse's bridal, and there we would sit, me legging on what might as well have been a brown and white spotted couch. After a few unsuccessful attempts at legging him forward, my instructor would pull out the crop—a 12-inch baton with a small paddle at the end. Then the most fascinating thing would happen: she would look the horse in his giant brown eye and say, "Okay, I'm giving her the crop." She'd hand me the crop, and the horse would start to walk.

Responsible horse trainers and riders know that you never whack a horse with the crop. Not only is it mean, it's unnecessary.

Gentle pressure can be applied to the side of the horse to mimic stronger leg power, which tells the horse to go forward. Over time, the horse learns that whoever has the crop has the authority. That's why my instructor could even just pretend to pass me the crop and underneath me four hooves would start to move.

The team leader, governance leader, and others elected to the governance board and council, must have authority over their domains. A title like "chief" or "director" certainly bolsters credibility. But title-based authority by itself is brittle. Strong authority takes an explicit endowment—a handing over—of authority whether you're on a data team or in the saddle.

Finally, the team leader **must have access to resources.** I knew a person who was hired in a data role but wasn't provided access to any of the organization's data. That must have been a frustrating experience for them, and, ultimately, a waste of money for the organization. If you know you will not be successful without a particular resource, your first and only job is to secure that resource. Can you do this job with no budget? Can you do it without executive buy-in? Can you do it without people? Without specific software? It's probably safe to say that nearly every manager wishes they had more resources. The key idea here is that certain resources—budget, executive buy-in, access to data, etc.—are required. To ensure you have those, develop a strong bottom line, as well as a slate of alternative projects and initiatives depending on the type of investment your company's leadership is willing to make.

As I hope you are now convinced, a certain title or place within the organization does not guarantee the success (or failure) of the data team leader or the team itself. If you are in the position of hiring someone to lead the data team, take stock of the factors discussed above. Where can this role fit that they will be set up for success? If you are the person being hired, get your leadership's honest assessment of the environment you are wading into. If you a member of the team, this section still applies to you. You too will be most successful if you have access to resources and autonomy over your work.

Hire #2: A Data Governance Leader

As children, many of us learn to consider how different experiences can lead to different interpretations of the world through the parable of "The Blind Men and the Elephant."[20] It goes like this:

Long ago six old men lived in a village in India. Each was born blind. The other villagers loved the old men and kept them away from harm. Since the blind men could not see the world for themselves, they had to imagine many of its wonders. They listened carefully to the stories told by travelers to learn what they could about life outside the village.

The men were curious about many of the stories they heard, but they were most curious about elephants. They were told that elephants could trample forests, carry huge burdens, and frighten young and old with their loud trumpet calls. But they also knew that the Rajah's daughter rode an elephant when she traveled in her father's kingdom. Would the Rajah let his daughter get near such a dangerous creature?

Finally, the villagers. . .arranged for the curious men to visit the palace of the Rajah to learn the truth about elephants.

When the blind men reached the palace. . .their friend led them to the courtyard. There stood an elephant. The blind men stepped forward to touch the creature that was the subject of so many arguments.

The first blind man reached out and touched the side of the huge animal. "An elephant is smooth and solid like a wall!" he declared. "It must be very powerful."

The second blind man put his hand on the elephant's limber trunk. "An elephant is like a giant snake," he announced.

The third blind man felt the elephant's pointed tusk. "I was right," he decided. "This creature is as sharp and deadly as a spear."

The fourth blind man touched one of the elephant's four legs. "What we have here," he said, "is an extremely large cow."

The fifth blind man felt the elephant's giant ear. "I believe an elephant is like a huge fan or maybe a magic carpet that can fly over mountains and treetops," he said.

The sixth blind man gave a tug on the elephant's coarse tail. "Why, this is nothing more than a piece of old rope. Dangerous, indeed," he scoffed.

"An elephant is like a wall," said the first blind man. "Surely we can finally agree on that."

"A wall? An elephant is a giant snake!" answered the second blind man.

"It's a spear, I tell you," insisted the third blind man.

"I'm certain it's a giant cow," said the fourth blind man.

"Magic carpet. There's no doubt," said the fifth blind man.

"Don't you see?" pleaded the sixth blind man. "Someone used a rope to trick us."

Their argument continued and their shouts grew louder and louder.

"Wall!" "Snake!" "Spear!" "Cow!" "Carpet!" "Rope!"

"Stop shouting!" called a very angry voice.

It was the Rajah, awakened from his nap by the noisy argument.

"How can each of you be so certain you are right?" asked the ruler.

The six blind men considered the question. And then, knowing the Rajah to be a very wise man, they decided to say nothing at all.

"The elephant is a very large animal," said the Rajah kindly. "Each man touched only one part. Perhaps if you put the parts *together, you will see the truth. Now, let me finish my nap in peace."*

Note that in the parable, the Rajah didn't urge the men to agree on which of their interpretations were correct. He encouraged them to consider that their perspectives might all be correct and, indeed, taken together describe an elephant. In this book, I will talk at length about the importance of standards, developing a shared organizational language, and managing exceptions. But we shouldn't rush to erase all nuance. At first glance, beauty marks can look like blemishes.

Consider different departments using the same term in different ways. It might be that the term sprouted up organically in each department, and no kernel of similarity underlies the definitions. Or it may be that the core definition of the term is consistent, but the departments vary in how they apply the term. In the second instance, you must define for the organization what the base term means, and then clearly document how the term might be used in different contexts. The goal here is to reduce noise while preserving differences that serve a legitimate business purpose. A skilled data governance leader can effectively strike this balance.

That's why the second hire on the list is a person to lead data governance. This role should work across the organization—both vertically and horizontally. The person filling this role must have the experience, influence, and freedom to navigate the expanse of this job. Does this mean that a junior person who is truly stellar can't come in and succeed? No. Does it mean that they must have years of experience in data governance or they will fail? No.

A data governance leader may be one of the more challenging roles to fill successfully because you are looking for a hybrid of sorts. The data governance leader needs to know both the business and they need to know the data. They need to be excellent change agents, mediators, and problem solvers. They need to have both the creativity to develop novel solutions and the discipline to implement them. They need to have a thick skin and abundant empathy. This is a hard job. Then, of course, they also inherit all of the "musts haves" of the chief or director: clout, authority, and resources.

Hiring Internally or Externally

One final consideration to think about when hiring a chief data officer and a data governance leader, as well as the rest of the team: should you hire from within or go for an external candidate? Like everything else, it depends.

Things to think about when hiring an internal candidate

Hiring from within is great because you'll have a person who has tons (hopefully) of institutional knowledge and has (again, hopefully) built great relationships with their colleagues. Also, others within the organization may have experience telling them to be defensive, territorial, or suspicious of an outsider.

But in some environments, even a qualified internal candidate may not be the best person for the job. First, if you've got a real silo problem in your organization, consider how hiring someone from one of the silos might affect the willingness of other existing departments to collaborate. ("I didn't want to share this data with you when you were in marketing, and I don't want to share it with you now.")

Further, how might hiring this hypothetical person affect the neutrality and objectivity with which a data team must operate? Will they be willing to see faults in systems they may have helped create? Will they be willing to tell their former teammates hard things? This is not to paint the picture that an internal candidate will always suffer from these effects. Indeed, even within my own organization, we've hired several internal candidates that are knowledgeable, clear-eyed, and well respected by their colleagues. I only mean to highlight the importance of inter-team dynamics here and encourage you to consider that in your hiring decisions.

Things to think about when hiring an external candidate

On the other hand, an external candidate will undoubtedly take longer to understand how the organization runs and all of its quirks and, as mentioned, those within the organization may feel resentful or suspicious of an outsider. But an external candidate can counteract these potential downsides by coming into the organization without any earned bias toward the company's current way of working. An external candidate's diversity of experience could also help the organization visualize new methods of operating and avoid learning some lessons the hard way.

Who had "synergy" on their business-jargon bingo board? Identifying Other Roles to Fill

You don't need me to tell you how important, yet difficult, it is to build a team that works almost effortlessly together. Even in the age of new roles, old rules still apply. To be successful, a team and its members should have clearly defined goals with expressly assigned duties.

Identifying Key Functions

If data management is a new function for you and your

organization, you'll be forgiven for looking at all eleven pieces of the DAMA wheel (refer to the earlier section "Pieces of a Wheel: The Importance of Data Governance") and wondering which functions can realistically be grouped together under one role. When assigning duties, be wary of a couple of potentially problematic patterns: over-specializing and over-generalizing.

Over-specializing

Over-specializing looks something like hiring a manager for data governance, a manager for master data management, a manager for metadata management, and a manager for data quality. To be sure, this route is not always the wrong move. But speaking specifically of the time period where you are building the program and getting your feet under you, hiring this many specialists is akin to having too many cooks in the kitchen. Why? Data governance, master data, metadata, and data quality management are related enough that separating them could create a scenario where your managers are working at cross purposes.

For example, suppose your initial goal is to identify and describe your company's critical data. In a purist sense, identifying and perfecting critical data is a main goal of a master data team; agreeing to definitions of terms is a function of data governance; both a term's status as critical data and its definition are metadata; data quality standards are typically set and enforced by data governance, but guaranteed by a master data function. You could, in theory, separate each of these functions. But consider starting small and consolidating this work in one or two key teams, at least early on, to avoid unnecessary complexity.

Over-generalizing

On the other hand, over-generalizing causes problems of its own. This pattern is less about grouping too many slices of the wheel together (although that could also create issues) and more about bestowing someone with a title that indicates little about their responsibilities. For example, Data Program Manager, or Manager of AI Innovation may well be positions that do a lot of important work. But, just by looking at the titles, what would you say belongs in the purview of each of these roles? Is the Data Program Manager more business focused or technology focused? Do they mainly deal with the care and maintenance of the organization's data? Or are they tasked with building data products, like dashboards? And what about our Manager of AI Innovation? Who else would this person have to rely on to do their job well? Attendant with the lack of clarity in these roles' titles is the fact that confusion will invite competition. Competition doesn't necessarily have to be adversarial, but it could mean that several people end up doing the same work.

Also consider how the rest of the organization would interact with your team. If you over-specialize and someone has a question about inconsistent field names, for example, they will have to decide whether to contact the data governance manager, or the data quality manager, or the master data manager. Don't put that burden on your colleagues or your customers. After all, these are probably new concepts to them as well.

Align – Build – Connect – Deliver

A failure to adequately describe and assign work can really weigh your team down. But we can arrive at success from many paths, and you certainly don't have to get it right the first time. In the beginning, my team fell slightly along the over-specialized line. Noticing more friction than we would have liked, we took another look at our strategy and asked ourselves what we really wanted to provide to the firm. We eventually settled into roles that fell along four major themes: **align, build, connect,** and **deliver** (Figure 6).

Instead of hiring someone "to implement a data

virtualization platform," we looked for someone who could **connect** people and systems with data while optimizing technical performance. Instead of looking for someone who could "write policies," we sought a person who could **align** our activities with the needs of the business. Of course, the job descriptions still need to be specific enough that people know what is expected of them. But giving each role a general theme leaves enough room to develop that functionality beyond its original construct, while minimizing the actual and theoretical overlap between roles.

ALIGN	BUILD	CONNECT	DELIVER
Institute policies, procedures, and standards. Lead data stewards, Council, and Board. Ensure data security, quality, and privacy.	Design and build physical data models and warehouses that convert raw data into formats supporting analytics.	Provide unified and simple access to data. Future-proof data connectivity.	Develop interactive dashboards conveying complex insights in an engaging and compelling manner.
Governance	Engineering	Virtualization	Analytics

Figure 6

Creating a Guiding Coalition

In his book *Leading Change*, change management researcher John P. Kotter identifies eight mistakes organizations make in their change efforts. After "underestimating the difficulty of forcing change," Kotter placed a "failure to create a sufficiently powerful guiding coalition" at the top of his errors list.[21] A multidisciplinary group of volunteers from across the organization, your guiding coalition advises on and helps implement your data strategy. This coalition is key to ensuring your projects align to what the business finds valuable and—if chosen carefully—can bolster the credibility of your team's work.

Luckily, Kotter advises us on how to carefully choose our coalition. First, he warns us against the scenario of "The Low Credibility Committee."[22] This scenario arises when our coalition doesn't sufficiently represent senior and executive company leaders. If senior leaders don't participate, the rest of the organization could easily reason that either the coalition lacks authority to decide important issues, or perhaps that this data initiative isn't really all that important.

Kotter urges us to instead seek out the following four characteristics of "high credibility" coalitions.

1. **Position Power**—those who are included in the coalition have sufficient sway such that those who are not included in the coalition can't block forward progress.

2. **Expertise**—members of the coalition have enough knowledge of their domain and of the organization to guard the coalition from any blind spots.

3. **Credibility**—those chosen to be part of the coalition have good reputations within the company.

4. **Leadership**—coalition members are known leaders in the company, making them key players in managing change.

By describing in Chapter 1 the various operating models, I have already given you a taste of how you might develop your guiding coalition. Expanding on that now, you can see how you might implement Kotter's advice in Figure 7. Given the magnitude of a data strategy and the amount of change expected, it is common to implement a three-tiered coalition. This type of tiered system consists of data stewards, a data governance council, and a data governance board.

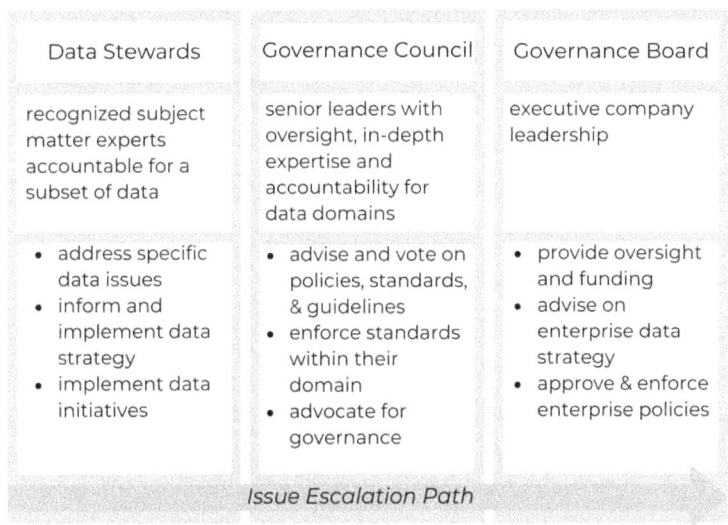

Figure 7

Heeding Kotter's advice, the members of your council and board should be directors and chiefs, respectively. As such, they imbue the coalition with position power, credibility, and leadership. Further, don't just include directors and chiefs from the technology side. Your council and board should consist of leaders from every major department in the company, like human resources, diversity & inclusion, marketing, finance, and, yes, technology. Inclusion of each business unit allows your coalition to operate from complete expertise.

Not only does building a strong coalition like this improve your team's chances of early success, it sustains what you've achieved. Not to steal too much thunder from Chapter 4, but your chances of sustained success are higher now that you have a key group of people in the organization who won't want to see the collapse of something they've helped create.

CHAPTER THREE
Happy Data

When people envision their companies operating with a best-in-class data estate, some might picture their colleagues scrolling through dashboards that rival those in *Minority Report*. I like to think we can keep the dashboards and avoid the dystopian, tech noir vision of America displayed in *Minority Report* if we envision our data's formative years a little differently.

What if we allowed our data to grow up like a teen in idealized mid-century middle-America, where the characters are quirky and the problem-solving is community based? Could we develop our capabilities—and our thinking—by anchoring to a system of values? Could we create a predictable safety net, one where folks can turn if they have a data issue or spot an opportunity? Could we create a coalition that collaborates on company data initiatives—and maybe even has a little fun? Might our data be less likely to turn on us if we do? I like to think so. By reading this chapter and completing the prompts, you can start to create that system of values, that safety net, that coalition that will sustain a responsible data program. At the end of this chapter, you will be able to:

- ✓ Describe the types of data governance and identify the type that is right for your organization
- ✓ Prepare for probing conversations with those in the organization
- ✓ Define the goals and guiding principles for your data governance program
- ✓ Confidently name eight types of data quality issues
- ✓ Quantify quality issues
- ✓ Understand and apply the basic principles of privacy and security
- ✓ Fortify your data handling ethics with knowledge of common fallacies and biases

All Roads Lead to Rome—and Data Governance

As you know from Chapter 1, data governance is the center and scaffolding of the data management wheel. Thus, no matter which data management functions you prioritize, your program must have a data governance arm. Data governance drives an organization's most valued objectives by managing the quality, availability, usability, and understandability of its strategic and critical data. As a central figure in drafting strategy and delivering value, the data governance leader must build robust, scalable policies and procedures and an engaged community of stakeholders.

Data as a business asset

Recall from Chapter 1 the distilled definition of data management and data governance: "data management (governance) is the recognition that data is an asset." To bolster your chances for creating a successful data management program, I'd like to refine this definition one more time. According to both research and experience, successful data management and governance programs succeed not just because they treat data like an asset. They succeed because they treat data like a business asset.

What's the distinction? With this twice-adjusted definition, I propose treating data as a business asset, rather than as a primarily technical asset. Historically, the prevailing schools of thought advocated for approaches that closely align control and management of data assets to control and management of IT assets. Some even suggest avoiding conversations with people in the business in favor of combing through data warehouses and other systems to see what is really going on with the data. To be sure, these activities are valuable and, indeed, critical to understanding "what is." But technology-led governance alone misses what we want "to be." Technology-led governance alone might tell you the "what," but it misses the "why." It misses the "how." It misses the "what next?"

Several books and articles talk about technology-led governance, so there's no need for us to spend a lot of time describing that specific framework. Instead, the remainder of this section shows how to build a data management and governance framework that is technology-enabled, but business-led.

Principles of business-led data management

You may have guessed that business-led data management and governance means putting the business, rather than the technology, at the center of your data management strategy. Like a lot of things in life, that's easy to say and hard to do. If you remember the following key principles, however, you will ensure a business-centric approach.

It's your job to understand how the company defines value

With several disciplines (see the section "Pieces of a Wheel: The Importance of Data Governance" from Chapter 1) and enumerable potential projects that could fall under the data management umbrella, it is critical that you narrow your scope of work to that which has a direct tie to business value. Though your business will surely have a documented strategy, that may not always be specific enough to inform a data strategy. Luckily, you can use the many sections throughout this book that focus on defining business value to fill in the gaps.

Accountability starts with the business users, not IT staff
Filling your data governance board, council, and steward positions with folks from the lines of business is not simply an act of goodwill. Those in the lines of business are the consumers and producers of the data and, as such, define what the data means and how it can be used. Given their knowledge of, and proximity to, the business data, they must be the first ones accountable for maintaining the standards developed in coordination with the data governance team. IT staff should act as support, ensuring availability of systems and correcting data on the backend where necessary.

Data management reinforces the company's culture and compliance

Two things that almost always make it into a company's strategy document: culture and compliance with laws and regulations. Less often is there a direct acknowledgment of the role data management plays in supporting these two focuses. If your data is primarily closed off in its source system, available only to those in a single department, this reinforces a siloed company culture. On the other hand, the data team can promote a culture of collaboration and sharing by, for example, bringing people together to develop a data sharing hub with common definitions for all critical data.

Most large companies are now also under increased pressure to develop policies relating to data privacy and use of artificial intelligence. Especially where data management is a new function at a company, the business's lawyers or risk management team may take total ownership of compliance with regulations and obligations. But, as a data leader, you can provide tremendous value in supporting compliance goals. Keep reading for more on how the data team can partner with risk and security teams to promote compliance.

No one is too technology-illiterate to use data

The final principle for business-led data management stands for the idea that every person should be able to enhance their work using data. People often tell me they don't pay attention to data because they aren't "tech-savvy" or they don't have a "math brain." I don't buy it.

It is part of the data team's job to make data understandable and accessible to non-technical users. This means that it is your job to make the technology as simple as possible and provide the right training and support so that no one is left behind. There will always be those who are intimidated by changes to their way of working. But I truly believe everyone can become data literate. Besides, the stakes are too high for some parts of the business to sit on the sidelines. For the company to reach its strategy—and data—goals, everyone must participate.

Business-led data management principles in action: starting your data governance strategy

In my firm, the data governance function is part of a larger data management team working to implement a centralized data hub. The goal of the data hub is to simplify system-to-system data integrations, create a curated data zone with role-based access to content, increase understandability of our data with a comprehensive data catalog, promote usability of our data with exceptional master data and data quality, and provide on-demand and custom visualization and analytics. The data governance team supports these goals by managing the community, literacy, standards, and security necessary for success.

Much in the same way we discussed strategy building in Chapter 1 (refer to the section "What would culture eat for breakfast during a strategy famine?"), I started building a data governance strategy by speaking with people and learning about the culture and priorities of the firm. I met with folks from every department, from chief to individual contributor.

Initially, we talked about everything but data. I found in my previous experience that, once someone knew my job title, they would start to filter their conversations with me to things they thought I would want to hear. When I worked in an innovation role, I would ask a lawyer what their biggest focus was at that moment; they would usually respond with a process that needed improved or a task they thought could be automated. I knew good and well this wasn't really their biggest focus. But it's what they figured I wanted to talk about. In a data-focused role, were I to ask a colleague what their current priority is, they would most likely respond by describing a dashboard or set of data they would like to have. Eventually, specific data requirements will be important, but relying solely on these types of answers might set you on a path of solving a problem that isn't preeminently important to your audience.

I found certain questions were better at drawing out responses that would help me better understand the firm, synthesize common pain points among departments and prioritize a body of work. When you are in discovery mode, try asking questions like these of the individuals you are interviewing:

- How ready to collaborate are folks within the organization?
- Do you think the organization has a silo problem? If so, how big do you think the problem is?
- Which resources at the organization do you personally find most helpful?
- Which other department does your department typically collaborate the most with?
- What are the main activities of your department?
- Tell me about the projects you are working on.
- Who are the top 3-5 people in the organization you go to when you have questions?

With these insights and those in your strategy draft from Chapter 1 (refer to the section "Components of a good data strategy"), you are in a good position to think specifically about your data governance mission, vision, and strategy.

Putting business-led principles to work

At this point, you have a lot of information you need to distill into a mission, vision, and strategy. You have the company-specific research you gathered here and in Chapter 1 (refer to section "...than at the end? Building a Case Your Organization Will Embrace"). You have structural guidance from the DAMA-DMBOK, lessons from Gartner, and business-led best practices from this book. Based on what you know a data team does, and what you know your company needs, what is your mission and vision for your team? Why, in other words, does your team exist? How do you want to be able to describe your team in five years?

Your mission and vision are your long-term, directional

goals, so you want to be specific, but not necessarily prescriptive (that will come later). I like to pair mission and vision statements with other themes that will provide a North Star when the path forward is unclear. Together, your mission, vision, and themes (or values) become the guiding principles for your more specific body of work.

Read the following example of guiding principles I drafted for my first data governance strategy (see "Insight: Example Data Governance Guiding Principles"). Notice how they elicit an image, not just of what my company is currently like, but of where we intend to go. In other words, you can sense the identity of the organization, but you can also clearly see the future of the firm. Pulling the thread from the organization's past to its future is a change management feature too often overlooked. Bake it into your strategy and notice how much simpler prioritizing and gathering support become.

Insight:

Example Data Governance Guiding Principles

Our mission—To make our firm the model of a modern, data-intelligent enterprise for law firms and legal departments around the world by focusing on transparency, authenticity, clarity, and consistency in everything we do.

Our vision—We are outcome-enablers, helping people achieve their business objectives through data. We operate like The Big Four accounting firms, like trailblazing consulting firms, like our most innovative clients, so that every employee and client views us as the gold-standard law firm for data intelligence and innovation.

Non-Invasive Data Governance—Our strategy is based in part on Robert Seiner's "Non-Invasive Data Governance" framework. This framework recognizes that our domain experts are already doing data governance work, whether they realize it or not. Rather than try to work against them and override how they are used to working, we will develop policies together with our existing business experts so that they are not "governed" but empowered to do their best work.

Community Marketplace—Our data team strives to create a community marketplace—a place to break down the barriers of understanding between departments and provide a space where people can collaborate to take their work to the next level. Sure, we could all remain local artisans and keep our insights to ourselves. But, like vendors at the Pike Place Market in our hometown of Seattle, our community knows that coming together is not just better for each of us, it's better for all of us.

Everyone can be data-intelligent—Just like everyone can learn to read if time is invested to help them learn, everyone can understand what we mean by "data," how to translate their business needs into data requirements, how to read and generate reports, and how our data, like any other asset, must be managed before it can be optimized.

Why this works: The principles I defined above worked well for my company for a few reasons. First, the firm was fairly technologically progressive as compared to many law firms, partially to retain its status as counsel to the world's most innovative companies (and partially because it's just good business). Our data governance mission and vision support and extend this broader identity of the firm. Second, I found the people at the firm were ready—enthusiastic, even—about collaborating to organize our data. But the roads of commerce were not yet open. Creating structured and unstructured means of communication, bringing as many people into the process as possible, unlocked doors that had previously been shut to meaningful partnership.

Next create short-term goals and roadmaps that break your broad guiding principles down into tangible, aspirational steps and address the primary pain points you discovered in your research and in conversations with the business.[23] Check out "Insight: Example Data Governance Short Term Goals and Roadmap" for an illustration of what your roadmap could include.

INSIGHT:

Example Data Governance Short Term Goals and Roadmap

Over the next two years, the data governance team will engage in specific activities that will build our credibility, sustainability, and value proposition. We will begin in Level 1 ("L1") where we will focus on building the core capabilities needed to mature to higher levels of analytics and automation. For this reason, we call this maturity level "Level 1: Core" or simply "Core" (see Figure 8). The strategic roadmap that follows outlines how we will reach Level 2 ("L2") by the end of the third quarter of next year.

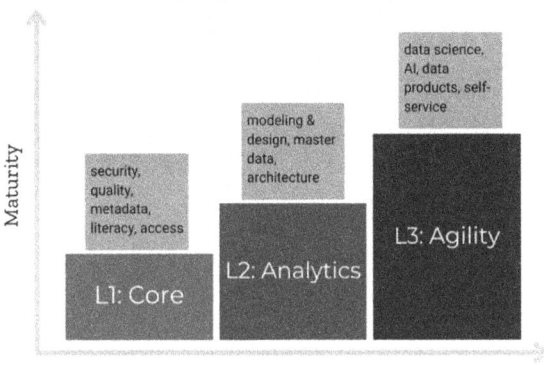

Figure 8

Drive business values and outcomes—we will ensure an airtight alignment between data governance projects and the firm's stated business objectives, and how investments in data governance positively impact these objectives. To accomplish this, we will:

- Complete a data strategy and readiness assessment to understand the firm's key priorities and how data supports them. We will use this information to form working groups and engagement plans with key stakeholders of these priorities.
- Engage our data governance board, council, and data stewards through intentional communication, tactical working groups, supportive education, and job aids, and by continuously showing tangible results.
- Focus on projects and data with a high return of investment.
- Track metrics that allow us to view our investments versus return.

- Develop organizational touch points to stay on top of developing business needs and opportunities.

Define accountability and decision rights—through standards, policy setting, and an educated firm, we will reduce friction and increase security, usability, and quality of our critical data. We will:

- Secure decision-making authority for our data governance board and council.
- Ensure lockstep coordination between the board and council.
- Empower and support data stewards with clear, proactive, and repeatable workflows.
- Monitor and measure data quality and policy compliance.

Operate with transparency and ethics—we will make governance decisions and recommendations with reference to agreed ethical data handling standards, and we will test our business and technical implementations for conformance with these rules. We will:

- Draft ethical data handling principles for board and council approval.
- Make ethical data handling part of our data literacy program.
- Build ethical data handling principles into policies, workflows, and technical resources to the extent necessary and possible.
- Maintain an inventory of all governed data assets.

Prioritize education and training—we will make data literacy a key part of the firm's culture by helping people articulate the importance of data quality, draw correct inferences using data analysis, and understand basic terminology. We will:

- Create a data literacy training program for all staff.
- Provide data coaching services or buddy systems.
- Advocate for building data literacy into core competencies.

Embed Data Governance into firm culture—we want our people to understand the role they—and their departments—play in leveraging data governance. We will work with our data governance partners throughout the firm to invest in communication, change management, and engaging multimedia content.

Why this works: It considers the goals of the firm, but also addresses the most common reasons governance efforts fail. It is specific and directional. Achievement of these items is easily measured. Most importantly, it shows that change will not happen overnight, but we have a plan.

The Data Governance Lifecycle

With some of the strategizing behind us, let us now look to how data governance often plays out in practice. Understanding the lifecycle of governance projects can help you not only manage each project effectively, but also help you decide what gets governed and at what level. In my experience, the lifecycle of a typical data governance initiative centers around six primary phases: Intake, Evaluate, Plan, Pilot, Implement, and Communicate. These phases are discrete, with people, processes, and tools supporting each.

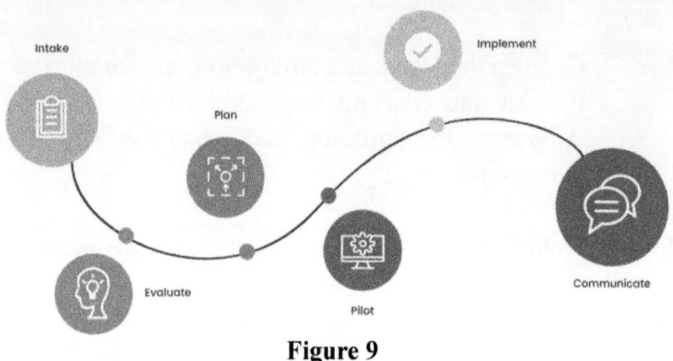

Figure 9

Of course, the image of the data governance lifecycle in Figure 9 is an idyllic abstraction of the true process. In reality, the lifecycle looks more like what is shown in Figure 10:

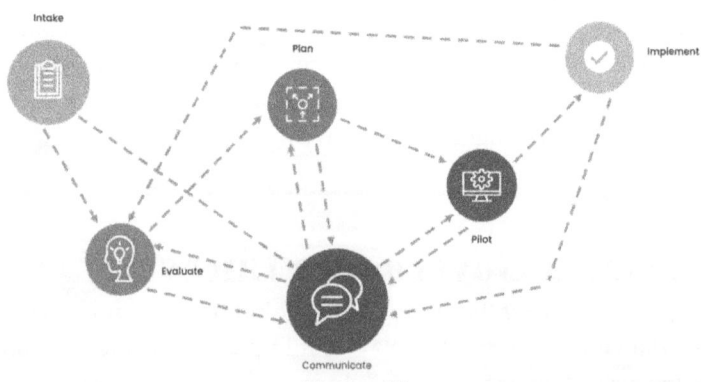

Figure 10

Not only is the reality of the second picture completely okay, it's preferred. An organization is a complex, non-linear system. Recognizing this, it's best to build flexibility into your processes. Crucially, what is also depicted in Figure 10 is a feedback mechanism whereby you can formalize learning and continuously engage your community. Notwithstanding their interconnectedness, the phases in and of themselves are distinct. I will give a brief overview of the phases here, but you can learn much more about each throughout the rest of this book.

Phase 1: Intake

The **Intake** phase begins by receiving issues or opportunities related to a specific data asset. While it's important to create specific processes around issue collection, a large part of gathering issues will likely be a result of talking with others and keeping an ear to the ground. That said, anyone in the company should be able to submit an issue related to data management to the data team. When you first start out, you might find it easiest to field issues and requests via email or through a spreadsheet collaboration platform like SmartSheets, Google Sheets, or Microsoft Excel Online. As you mature, you can manage issues directly through a data catalog. Next in the Intake phase, you should triage the submission using a number of factors, including whether a team other than data governance should own the issue. The purpose of this phase is to properly prioritize and resource the submitted issue, though recording issues and opportunities in this way benefits other phases as well.

Phase 2: Evaluate

You may enter the **Evaluate** phase a few different ways: after intake of a new issue, after completing a pilot, or as part of ongoing data quality audits. The goals of this phase are to uncover all sides of an issue, hear from stakeholders, ensure you progress as expected, and remain agile in your approach. You can learn more about our evaluation tools and processes in Chapter 5.

Phases 3-5: Plan, Pilot, and Implement

Plan, **Pilot**, and **Implement** are intensive yet critical phases of the data governance lifecycle. Many of the aspects of these phases are beyond the scope of this book. But I want to spend a few words on the reason I include these as distinct phases. If you are reading this book, you are likely familiar with piloting software before implementing it. Equally important, though not often done, is piloting a process, metric, or method before investing in full implementation. Piloting is as much a change management concept as it is a test of efficacy. If folks know that you are testing a well-reasoned guess as to what might best solve a problem, and that you are willing to try other things that may work better, they are much likelier to join the efforts as helpers rather than hostages. Piloting can be complex, but the main idea is to show people you respect their resources by asking them to go all-in on an idea only after you've vetted on a small scale.

Phase 6: Communicate

Finally, **Communicate** to inform, to persuade, to gain support, to give support, and to collaborate. Like non-technical pilots, communication and change management are often underutilized. In the legal industry, we experience a strange phenomenon where our email inboxes are always overflowing, yet we never feel fully informed. My guess is that the legal industry is not alone in this feeling. I've tried to tackle this problem by building a communication and change management strategy that focuses on targeted, multi-modal content. I'll detail this in Chapter 6.

Deciding What Gets Governed

You should now be able to visualize the broad strokes of data governance structure and activities. At this point, though, you may be wondering exactly what gets "governed." Most of this depends on the priorities you identified here and in Chapter 1. Part of it depends on the resources you have to get started. And the rest largely depends on how you want to grow.

Where to start

Using the maturity model in Figure 8, I suggest planning work by asking what needs to be done in order to reach each level of maturity (see Figure 11).

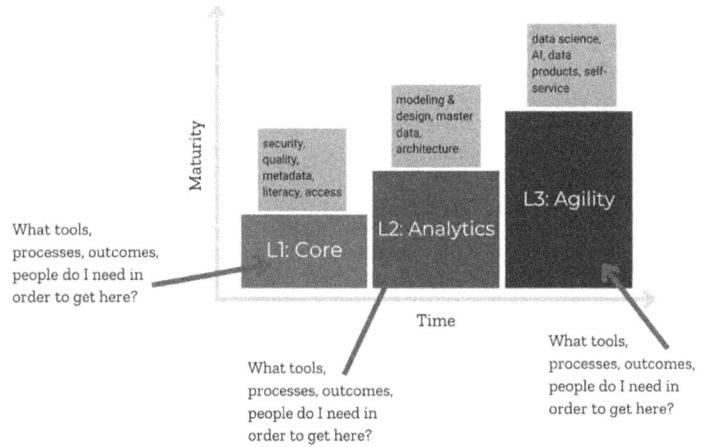

Figure 11

During this process, I encourage you to take an honest assessment of where you need to start versus where you want to start. In my experience, organizations will often try to start at Level 2 (or even Level 3) because they see analytics and agility as the value-add. I have even heard Level 1 initiatives like data quality described as the "un-sexy cousin" of analytics, "boring," "impossible," "a slog." In the best-case scenario, these Level-1-haters develop their Core even if they don't put it in a press release. In the worst-case scenario, the Core doesn't get built at all. We have all heard the maxim "garbage in, garbage out." Level 1 is where you determine whether your analytics and AI give you garbage.

Which data will you focus on?

Let's assume I've convinced you to start at Level 1. You now need to decide which data you will subject to your efforts. The vast majority who undertake enterprise data management will find themselves, at one point or another, trying to manage "all the data." But if we agree that data management should align with the priorities of the business, then we have two paths to determining which data gets governed first: the bottom-up path and the top-down path.

The bottom-up path

You may find yourself along the bottom-up path if you're working without a clear mandate from your senior leadership. Maybe you are building a case for greater investment in data management, or maybe this is your pet project, born out of your own frustrations. Either way, without leadership direction, you may find yourself trying to manage all data. This will not get you where you want to go. If you are working from the bottom-up, you will have to decide which data to target.

You will find plenty of great resources online, in the DAMA-DMBOK, and in books like the one you're reading that suggest which foundational datasets to focus on first. But don't forget your richest source of inspiration: your own business. Your colleagues are a wealth of knowledge on the company's pain points. Go back to those questions I listed in the opening of this chapter. Even if you have been with your organization for a while, set aside your assumptions, and start these conversations at a high level with your colleagues. Then dig deeper into the data with them. You may want to ask:

- What data do you rely on to do your job?
- How easy is it to get that data?
- Is the data usually accurate and complete?
- What is the system of record for that data?
- Do other systems house this data? Do the data in these systems match the data in your system of record?
- Do you often combine this data with data from other sources?

From these conversations, patterns will start to emerge. You may notice that business units across the organization rely on, say, customer data. You also notice that many report customer data to be inconsistent, hard to access, or otherwise frustrating to work with. This sounds like a great set of data to master.

The top-down path

On the opposite end of the spectrum, you may have full leadership support and a clear mandate to clean up the organization's data. Perhaps you are one of the lucky few who were even given a clear direction from your C-Suite:

"Get rid of the duplicate entries in the financial system so we're not paying unnecessary storage costs!"

If you are one of the lucky ones, feel free to skip to the next section. If you're like the rest of us, you still have some work to do.

Having top-down support is not only critical to the success of the program, it ostensibly makes prioritizing projects easier. This doesn't necessarily mean, though, that your senior leaders will tell you exactly where to focus. Even if you get a hold of the organization's strategy document, you will likely find a number of priorities of seemingly equal weight. Rarely will a list of data requirements accompany these priorities.

Drilling down to the data level

Regardless of whether you start from the bottom-up or the top-down, your role is to uncover these data requirements through a process I refer to as "Organizational Archeology." As an Organizational Archaeologist, you will work with your leadership to identify the most fertile ground, and then you will excavate through the layers of sub-processes and systems, narrowing your focus, until you finally reach the data level, where you will uncover the precise data fields that need governed. The various layers look something like Figure 12.

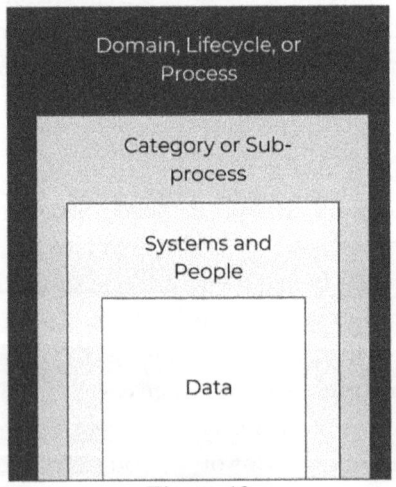

Figure 12

The domain, lifecycle, or process level

At the top layer is the primary domain, lifecycle, or process at issue.

- A "domain" is a subject area or particular category of data. For example, based upon your business, you may have a "People" domain, a "Customers" domain, a "Finance" domain, or even domains for each distinct line of business. We'll talk more about selecting your domains in Chapter 5.
- A "process" is, familiarly, a series of steps undertaken to achieve a defined goal.
- A "lifecycle" is a group of processes.

To illustrate the difference between these last two, you might consider the customer acquisition lifecycle as a series of processes: identifying your target market, performing SEO and marketing, and so on.

You might notice that you could make an argument for something being either a process or a lifecycle. I don't have a particular formula for selecting one over the other. I tend to define lifecycles as broadly as is reasonable, and then dig down into smaller sub-processes as necessary.

Once you identify the domain, lifecycle, or process that interests you, pause. What can you learn at this level? If you are looking at a specific lifecycle, for example, what are the outcomes? What is a beneficial or expected outcome? What is an adverse or unexpected outcome? What are the organization's goals for this particular lifecycle? Do they want to make it faster? More enjoyable?

The category or sub-process level

The second layer from the top is the category or sub-process of focus. A sub-process is, perhaps predictably, a process within a process, while a data category is a subset of a domain. Taking our "People" domain example, a category of this domain might be demographic data or job history data.

Again, pause: what can you learn at the category or sub-process level? If your stakeholders want to focus on demographic data, why? Is it of poor quality? Are they looking to stave off a leak of sensitive information?

The systems and people level

The next layer down is the systems and people layer. Because you've narrowed the scope of your focus, you are now in a position to identify the systems that store the data you're after, as well as the people who manage or consume that data.

What can you learn at this level? Who is responsible for the data in this category? Is that clear or unclear? In which system(s) does this category of data reside? Does it exist outside of systems, like in spreadsheets on someone's desktop?

The data level

Finally, the last layer to excavate is the data layer. This is where you pinpoint the exact fields of data you need to focus on to solve the problems your stakeholders initially raised. Because you've taken this layer-by-layer approach, you are at a significant advantage in identifying this data than had you started cold. But your excavation is not over. Not all of the data in this category is data that you need to govern right now to deliver results. At least, you likely don't need to govern it all at the same level. At this final layer, you will instead identify data that is critical to the process at issue, leaving a smaller subset of fields to asses for quality and utility.

Hopefully you are starting to see how, had you jumped straight into trying to govern the actual data, you could have cast too wide a net, spending unnecessary time trying to give structure to an amorphous blob.

Getting to the root causes of an issue: An Example

Let's walk through what this means with another example

from my work. You can see in Figure 13 that we were working from an initial consensus that we wanted to optimize our people data. In conversations with our data governance board and council, as well as others throughout the firm, we had received general feedback that the data we collected about our people (employees, partners, vendors, and contractors) was of poor quality or otherwise hard to use. The evidence we had to work with in the beginning was vague, but this was enough for us to get started.

Once we knew that the priority domain for our leadership was people data, we asked questions that would help us identify a smaller subset of that domain. We asked, for example, "does a particular category of people data concern you (for example, peoples' self-identified diversity characteristics)?" Or, "is there a certain process that you find especially unworkable (e.g., onboarding new employees)?" From this line of questioning, we gathered that the main problem was getting accurate reporting on things like total headcount and job history because, depending upon where one got the data, they might get different numbers.

This knowledge allowed us to dive deeper into the issues, identifying their root causes and understanding their histories. We asked which system(s) housed people data and who typically created and used the reports. Given that one of the main problems was the diverging headcount numbers, it came as no surprise that we had people data sitting in multiple systems. It lived in our HR system but had also meandered into our financial system and camped in local Excel files. This alerted us to the need to designate a system of record, as well as assign a person who would be accountable for maintaining this data.

Finally, we landed on the deepest layer of our discovery: the data. At this stage, we asked questions like: Which critical data is reported most frequently? What data is pulled most frequently into other systems? Which of the hundred-plus people data fields were most important to "get right"? Once we had our list of critical data, we asked a simple question: why is it problematic? A response like this was common: "well, because, all of my HR reports on headcount number agree with each other, but finance's numbers don't agree with mine." Now, that disagreement indicates one of two main possibilities: either there is a technical reason why the data doesn't match (for example, the data doesn't refresh at the same rate) or the two departments define the term "headcount" differently. Could one department perhaps include contingent workers in their definition while the other department considers only permanent employees?

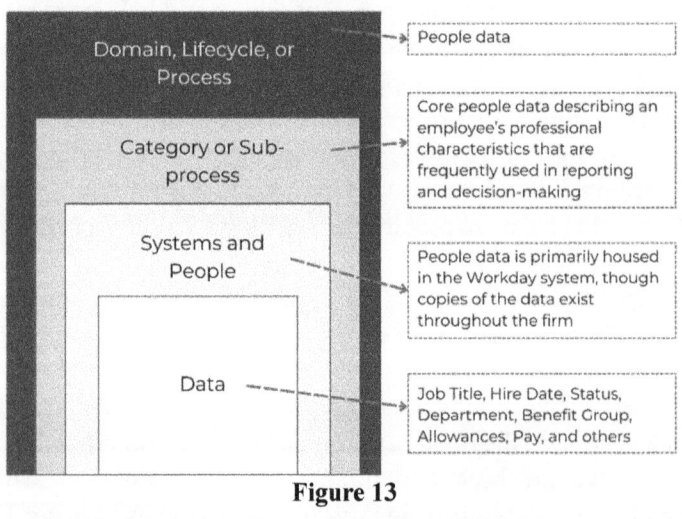
Figure 13

The 3 Ss of Data Governance

Throughout this Archeology project, we've uncovered something special: the "3 Ss" of Data Governance. Not particularly catchy, but it is easy to remember. What are the 3 Ss of Data Governance? To be appropriately governed, each piece of critical data needs a steward, a standard, and a system of record.

System of Record

A system of record—sometimes called "source of truth"—is the system chosen to store the most accurate version of certain data. Systems of record are critical to ensuring data is accurate, findable, and useable.

In my experience, folks usually agree about what the system of record should be for a category of data. That is, people tend to readily agree that data about employees should come from the HR system, financial data should come from the finance system, and so forth.

Problems usually arise because that data gets copied from the system of record into another system (or worse—a spreadsheet), where it may be transformed or stretched beyond its original purpose. Of course, this doesn't mean that data should never leave the source system. It will. But for data governance purposes, designating a system of record is, in essence, setting a policy that if we have two copies of the same data, whichever version matches the system of record is the correct version.

INSIGHT:

Phone Numbers and Fake News

Have you ever stopped to appreciate the extraordinary feat of data governance that goes into assigning telephone numbers? Each number can be assigned to one—and only one—person in the world. Each country has its own allowable number of digits and an accepted format. And we universally accept this system; does Verizon ever just decide to start assigning 20-digit phone numbers to its customers?

Nope. One string of 10 digits is universally accepted

as my phone number, just as one string of 10 digits is universally accepted as your phone number. Yet, you haven't fully lived until you've either heard or spoken the phrase, "Sorry, wrong number." Why? Two dynamics are at play. First, we have the people who intentionally spread fake news. Second, we have accidental fake news spreaders, made possible because a person is copying a phone number, rather than pulling it directly from a system of record. For our intentional fake news spreaders, a system of record is less important. If someone doesn't want us to have their phone number, we should probably just move on.

But the second dynamic illustrates why designating a system of record for critical data is paramount. Consider if we lived in a world with no national telephone registry. Phone numbers don't occur naturally. They aren't something we're born with. They aren't immutably attached to anything in the physical environment. Contrast this to something like eye color.

I don't care what any database says; my eyes are green. You can look at me and verify that statement. But without a designated, universally accepted national telephone registry, things would be chaos. Multiple people could have the same number. First responders couldn't trace calls. We'd have to assign 20-digit phone numbers because we would have no way of knowing if a phone number was available for reissue. So the next time you send a text to a phone number knowing your best friend will be on the receiving end, spare a moment of gratitude for the concept of a system of record.

Standard

A standard is any type of rule applied to a piece of data that people in the organization must follow, barring approved exceptions. This could include formatting standards, such as those that govern valid email address formats or password characters, but it could also include standard definitions, policies, or use cases. We will talk much more about standards in later chapters.

Steward

Finally, each piece of critical data needs a steward. Once you've done the hard work to define standards and systems of record for your data, someone will need to ensure compliance day-to-day. Revisit a data steward's responsibilities discussed in Figure 7 of Chapter 2. Now it's time for those stewards to shine.

Poor, Unfortunate Data

I once saw a LinkedIn post claiming that about 60 percent of data scientists' time is spent getting data into a usable format (a process often referred to as "data cleaning"). That means only 40 percent of their time is spent doing work we typically associate with a data scientist: building models to answer business questions, developing algorithms and applications, and simulating and optimizing the business environment. Assuming average salaries of $90,000 USD per year, an organization with 20 data scientists spends over $1 million USD every year cleaning data. But even businesses with few or no data scientists must use data—data which must also be in a usable format. If trained data scientists spend 60 percent of their time cleaning data, imagine how high this percentage is for those untrained in programmatic data cleaning.

Defining Good Data

One of my favorite sayings is "The great thing about standards is there are so many to choose from." This sentiment could equally apply to data quality frameworks. Indeed, the DAMA-DMBOK limited itself to covering only the three most popular.[24] As the DMBOK points out, though, most of the frameworks center around eight measures of data quality (even if they differ in their naming of the quality dimensions). For purposes of getting started, I encourage you to measure your data's quality against these eight dimensions, rather than getting wrapped up in a particular framework.

- **Accuracy:** the extent to which data correctly represents the real world, a system of record, or verified reference data (e.g., stock ticker symbols).
- **Completeness:** the degree to which the data contains all pieces required or expected.
- **Consistency:** the extent to which data values are represented in the same way within, and between, systems.
- **Integrity:** whether a data set has missing values, duplicates, invalid keys, or other technical issues that affect the utility of the set.
- **Reasonability:** whether the values of a data set or patterns in data over time meet our expectations based on what we know about the world (including our business). Highly unusual data might signal an issue with another data quality dimension, like accuracy.
- **Timeliness:** the extent to which data is available when a user needs it.
- **Uniqueness:** whether the same record exists more than once in a data set (also known as a "duplicate"). A lack of uniqueness could signal a data integrity issue.
- **Validity:** whether data values conform to a set of agreed values or range of values.

Dealing with inconsistent data: An Example

In the legal industry, law firms have unique identifiers for each client and for each matter worked on. We use these client-matter numbers to identify a piece of work for billing, conflicts, analysis, integration, and many other purposes. We use these numbers for so much that when I took on a project to clean up my organization's client-matter numbers, we found them living in 40 separate IT systems. In other words, client-matter numbers at my company (and, indeed, at law firms in general) are critical data.

The name alone tells us that "critical data" is that data which is core to the business. So, what data is core to the business? I've heard this type of data helpfully referred to as "connective tissue" or "grout between the tiles." This metaphorically describes data that:

- Is highly regulated or can pose a significant legal or ethical risk to the organization; AND/OR
- Has a high system impact (e.g., the data is used in greater than 40 systems); AND/OR
- Serves a strategic business objective for the organization

In practice, prioritizing some data over others is not always straightforward. Indeed, there is likely data that everyone in the organization agrees is important (e.g., personal addresses, profit and loss, etc.) but which does not rise to a level of criticality such that it should be the initial focus of enterprise governance.

If you are still unsure where to find the critical data in your organization, it may be helpful to look at your company's current business intelligence reporting to see which fields crop up the most often.

It's not a bad thing to have critical data in dozens of systems. But sprawling data is at greater risk for quality issues. In those 40 systems containing my company's client-matter numbers, for example, the numbers were formatted inconsistently in seven of the 40 systems. Both between and within systems, we saw five-digit client numbers separated from matter and child matter numbers by dashes, or six-digit client numbers separated from matter and child matter numbers by periods, or five-or-six-digit client numbers separated from matter and child matter numbers by both dashes and periods.

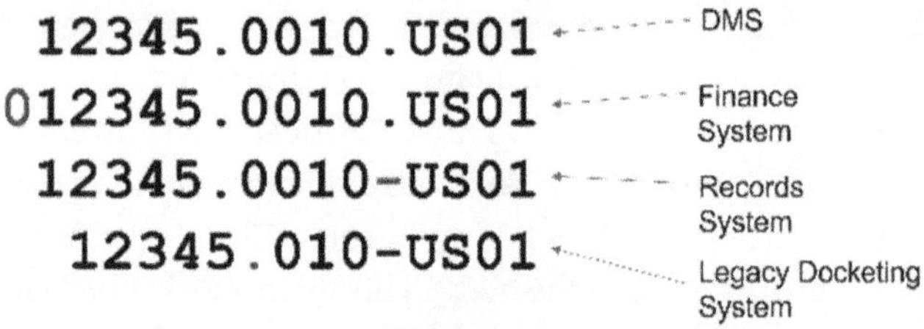

```
12345.0010.US01      ←------- DMS
012345.0010.US01     ←------- Finance System
12345.0010-US01      ←------- Records System
12345.010-US01       ←------- Legacy Docketing System
```

Figure 14

Why is this a big deal? From user-facing functions like search and analysis, to back-end functions like system integrations, mismatched identifiers are like gravel in gears. To keep the system running, any time the gears get gummed up, you have to stop the system, find the gravel, dust off that part of the gear, and hope you got it all before starting again. This takes time, and it takes money. And it's what balloons the time we spend cleaning data to 60 percent of our day.

Applying the Data Quality Dimensions

What I described in the example is an issue with the consistency data quality dimension. Consistency issues are incredibly common, and it wouldn't surprise me if you found yourself nodding along in sympathy with my example. To sharpen your quality issue spotting skills, refer to Table 2 below, read the prompts on the left and jot down examples of this phenomenon you see in your organization or your own life on the right.

Prompt	Your Example
Cite an example of data in your organization or life that did not match the authoritative source (the "truth"). For example, your street address is listed incorrectly on your bank statement. (Accuracy)	
Cite an example of data in your organization or life that did not contain all the required	

elements. For example, your street address is correct, but the city and state are missing. (Completeness)	
Cite an example of data values that differed within or between data sets. For example, dates in System A are formatted dd/mm/yyyy, while dates in System B are formatted Month Day, Year. (Consistency)	
Cite an example where you have seen mismatched key-value pairs. For example, in a law firm, we cannot open a matter without designating who the client is. A	

key-value pair issue would arise if we opened a matter in System A that could not be ascribed to any client (our key value). (Integrity)	
Cite an example where a particular data pattern did not meet expectations of reality. For example, if a data set showed that customers in Dallas bought more winter coats than customers in Chicago. (Reasonableness)	
Cite an example of a time when data changed more frequently than it became available to you. As an example, stock prices need	

to be available continuously throughout the day as they can change by the second. (Timeliness)	
Cite an example in your organization or personal life where a data value did not match the defined set of valid values. For example, when an online form asks for your phone number. If you type letters instead of numbers into the response field, you will receive an error. (Validity)	

Table 2

Through the above exercise, you probably found that you could have named multiple examples for certain quality dimensions, while others were more difficult to relate to. This is a good thing: it will help you define processes that identify and remedy the major sources of quality issues in your company. For example, perhaps ideas flowed freely when you filled out the first box as you cited examples of misspelled names, incorrect email addresses, or mislabeled accounts. In other words, your organization has a lot of inaccurate data. With this knowledge, you may then want to focus your quality projects on identifying the root causes of these accuracy issues. Could automation reduce typographical errors and mislabeling? Are automated systems pulling the data from a system that itself is inaccurate? Have you failed to designate a system of record for this data?

Raising Data Quality Levels: A Methodical Approach

Don't worry if you find yourself heavy on quality issues but light on resources. In the first couple of years of your data management journey, you may not need a formal data quality program to start cleaning up your data. Rather, you can use Organizational Archeology to identify your company's critical and priority data and focus on improving that key data.

Starting with the 3 Ss

Recall the inconsistencies in my client-matter number data (refer to the section "Dealing with inconsistent data: An Example). Because client-matter numbers are a critical piece of data for the firm, our group new it would pay big dividends to standardize it. To start this process, we tracked down every system that used client-matter data (either as a producer of the numbers or a consumer of the numbers). We brought this inventory to our data governance council, and we determined which of those 40 systems should be the system of record. That is, which system will have the "true" number against which all other systems should match. At this time, our council also recommended, voted on, and adopted a standard format for the numbers. Once we determined the system of record and the standard, we then went through our inventory of systems and flagged those that were out of compliance with the standard.

The previous steps allowed us to form a working group of all stewards of the secondary systems (i.e., the 39 other systems that are not the system of record). All I knew upon convening this group was that the systems had client-matter numbers that did not conform to our standard. I didn't know why, and because I didn't know why, I couldn't propose any concrete plans for fixing the mismatches. All I could do at the outset was to present a framework for how we'd get to where we needed to be.

Applying the Plan, Do, Check, Act (PDCA) model

In my first job after law school, I had a mentor named Jim Manley. Jim wasn't a lawyer—he didn't even work in law firms. But Jim was the expert in designing processes that consistently delivered high quality output. Jim had worked at General Motors for many years doing just that. He credited much of his success to having worked with W. Edwards Deming in his early career. Deming is a name you might recognize if you are familiar with the Plan, Do, Check, Act (PDCA) cycle he popularized in his pursuit of quality manufacturing. Although it started as a quality management tool for manufacturing, this continuous improvement cycle equally applies to service industries like law—as long as you follow its core tenant of being hard on the process but easy on the people. Having spent the years between my first job and my current job "winging" more projects than I'd care to admit to Jim, I returned to my old lessons and asked my new data quality working group to follow this PDCA process with me.

Plan

At the heart of the "Plan" step is to identify root causes of issues and draft a plan to address those root causes.[25] Some causes, we found, were purely technical (for example, a bit of code in the secondary system changed the format of the number when getting it from the source system). Other causes were procedural (e.g., people manually entered the number in their preferred format). Still others were a mix of technical and procedural causes.

Do

In the "Do" step, you execute your plan to address the root causes of the issues identified in the "Plan" phase. Knowing the root causes of our client-matter number inconsistencies and their techno-procedural nature, we applied a mix of technical and non-technical fixes as appropriate.

Check

In the "Check" step, you evaluate whether your interventions are working as you intended. Traditionally, the "Check" step involves calculating a quality score that measures defects as a percent of the total output (see "Insight: Calculating Data Quality"). For the client-matter number example, and for other quality remediation projects, it is helpful to calculate the data's current quality score, its likely quality score after remediation, and then its quality score at regular intervals after remediation. Tracking quality in this way allows you to demonstrate measurable value to your stakeholders, and to test whether quality dips in the future.

Act

The "Act" step is where you would fix any issues that arose in the "Check" step. Indeed, this is where the cyclical nature of the PDCA cycle becomes clear, as it is often necessary to return to the "Plan" step to understand the root cause of your findings.

Remember, you're not ever going to know everything you need to know about a quality issue at the beginning of the process. But inherent in the PDCA process is learning. That's what I hope you got from my example. If you are confident in your ability to solve problems, and if you stay true to the process, it's okay if you have to figure some things out along the way. Don't fear being the leader who tells your team, "It may not be fast, but we're going to work on hard problems, we're going to do it as a group, and we're going to experiment until we get it right." See if you don't end up making more progress that way in the end.

Insight:

Calculating Data Quality

One straightforward way to measure quality is to simply divide the expected or "good" output by the total output. This is commonly done in manufacturing (resulting in a measure called "Quality") and other hard sciences (where it is often called "Purity"). The "good divided by total" measure of quality works well as a quick snapshot of the overall health of the production line; however, I wanted a quality equation that I could use to (1) fully understand the depth of the quality issues and (2) more accurately predict the payoff for our remediation efforts. I therefore wrote a custom quality equation, whereby we could ascribe a current overall quality score to a data asset using eight quality dimensions:

where $\mathbf{Dim} = \mathbf{0}$ (quality issue not present) or $\mathbf{1}$ (quality issue present) for each of the n quality dimensions (accuracy, completeness, consistency, *integrity, reasonability, timeliness, uniqueness, validity)*

where N = *# of total systems using the data in question*

where **Depth** = $\frac{\text{\# of systems where Dim}=1}{N}$

where Q = *a data asset's quality score, reported as a percent*

let $Q = \frac{\sum_{i=1}^{n} Dim_i(1-Depth_i)}{n} \times 100$

When evaluating a data asset for quality improvement, the asset is then assigned an expected Quality score which represents the degree to which the asset's quality is expected to improve after remediation:

where $.95_t$ *represents a heuristic that a purely technical solution will result in the desired outcome 95% of the time*

where $.75_p$ *represents a heuristic that a pure process solution will result in the desired outcome 75% of the time*

where $\mathbf{Dim'_i} = 1 - Depth_i + Depth_i(.95_t + .75_p)$

let $Q' = \frac{\sum_{i=1}^{n} Dim'_i}{n} \times 100$

When to Focus on Data Quality

You may feel at this point that I am giving you mixed messages: I didn't mention data quality in the list of "must-haves" for a new data management program, yet I just devoted a whole section of this book to it. I told you that we didn't have a data quality program for the first two years of our department, yet I included data quality in Level 1 of our maturity model. So, what gives? Should you focus on data quality straight away or not? It depends.

It depends, in part, on whether we are talking about conducting a data quality project or if we are talking about implementing a data quality program. Similar to data governance, data quality is a discipline unto itself. And, because preventing, identifying, and correcting quality issues happens at every stage of the data life cycle, implementing a quality program requires thoughtful coordination with the other facets of your data management program. If you hope to do anything worthwhile with the data your organization produces, quality is essential.

If you are in a heavily regulated industry, for example, and your data must be complete, correct, and ready for audit at a moment's notice, please: prioritize data quality. But for many organizations, a measured pace that allows other data management disciplines to mature at the same time is best.

In my work, we chose not to initially focus on data quality—at least not directly. We reasoned that, since quality is decided by the condition of the other steps in the data life cycle, we could indirectly improve a lot of our data's quality by raising the quality of our other operations. For us, this meant a heavy focus on data governance and literacy. When the data governance team needed to intervene directly, we targeted high-impact quality improvement projects for our most critical data, like our client-matter data.

For us, this approach worked well because to our business, data quality was important, but not urgent. We were therefore able to take on quality projects at a slower pace. Furthermore, we saw an opportunity to enlist more folks to our cause by bringing our data quality issues to the fore, rather than trying clandestine efforts to fix them. Operating on the gamble that "sunlight is the best disinfectant," we prioritized making our data available.

Turns out, once people could see the real state of their data, we could barely keep up with the requests to fix it.

Data, and Other Intangibles: Privacy, Security, and Ethics

Privacy, security, ethics: three things we intrinsically know that we either have or we don't. But are each complex to define—and being hard to define, they can be challenging to protect.

INSIGHT:

A brief history and explanation of privacy rights

Supreme Court Justice Louis Brandeis (1856-1941), in advocating for an explicit right to privacy, gave us what is still probably the best definition of privacy. Speaking of the developing technologies of his day, Brandeis wrote[26] in 1890:

> "Recent inventions and business methods call attention to the next step which must be taken for the protection of the person, and for securing to the individual…the right 'to be let alone'…Numerous mechanical devises threaten to make good the prediction that 'what is whispered in the closet shall be proclaimed from the house-tops.'"

Even before Brandeis's day, US Constitutional Amendments touched on a person's right to privacy. First in the Fourth Amendment:

> *The right of the people to be **secure in their persons, houses, papers, and effects, against unreasonable searches and seizures**, shall not be violated, and no Warrants shall issue, but upon probable cause, supported by Oath or affirmation, and particularly describing the place to be searched, and the persons or things to be seized.*

And then in Section 1 of the Fourteenth Amendment:

> *All persons born or naturalized in the United States, and subject to the jurisdiction thereof, are citizens of the United States and of the state wherein they reside. No state shall make or enforce any law which shall abridge **the privileges or immunities of citizens of the United States; nor shall any state deprive any person of life, liberty, or property, without due process of law;** nor deny to any person within its jurisdiction the equal protection of the laws.*

The text of the Fourth Amendment is saying that wherever you might reasonably expect privacy—perhaps your home, your diary, your cell phone, your body—the government can intrude on that privacy only if they have a really good reason. This amendment is now the underpinning of United States Criminal Procedure, though the framers originally added it as a response to British Kings' non-criminal incursions into citizens' homes. While still the most plain-language example of privacy rights enshrined in our Constitution, courts have congealed around the opinion that the first and second clauses of that Amendment should be read together—that is, one is protected against unreasonable searches and seizures in a context where a warrant could be sought. In other words, in a criminal inquiry.[27]

The Fourteenth Amendment, on the other hand, is more ambiguous, but many of the privacy rights we enjoy today we have derived from the highlighted clauses. From these "Privileges and Immunities" and "Liberty" clauses, US courts have found a right to be free from governmental interference in certain personal affairs—for example, marriage, health care, and even possession of obscene materials.[28] These are just examples from the United States, but privacy rights have become a hallmark of a liberal democracy.

It is from foundational privacy rights, like the ones enshrined in the United States' founding documents and seminal Supreme Court decisions (see "Insight: A brief history and explanation of privacy rights" for details), several countries have developed legislation protecting digitally formatted private information (in other words: data). But before we move on to highlighting a few of these laws, I invite you to spend another moment in history. When the Framers wrote the Constitution 250 years ago, they didn't spend time writing the Fourth and Fourteenth Amendments because they were afraid that one day Facebook would try to sell our data. They gave us these words because they understood that the right to privacy is necessary for a person to be considered fully free. As the steward of peoples' private information, you protect one of their inalienable rights. I would thus caution against a check-the-box privacy and security approach and encourage you to lead with privacy rights always in mind.

A final word of caution as you move through this chapter: the privacy, security, and ethical landscape are ever-evolving. I will therefore focus mainly on the principles of privacy and security and examples of current legislation. This should give you a sense for the environment and help you develop an intuition about data privacy, security, and ethics. Please always coordinate with your privacy and security colleagues when managing sensitive information.

To be Let Alone: Protecting Personal Information

Given the discussion above, you may feel overwhelmed by the weight of your privacy obligations. But, to make explicit what you may have inferred, these obligations do not attach to all information. They apply only to personal information—data that can identify a person.

Quick Reference:

Personal Information: information that is or can be about or related to an *identifiable person*.

SOURCE: *General Accepted Privacy Principles (GAPP), American Institute of Certified Public Accountants (AICPA)*

The "identifiable person" designation tells us that information is considered personal only if you can identify the person the information describes. This includes data such as someone's name, social security number, or demographic information if the data set is small enough that a person in the group would be easily identified by their demographics. Sufficiently aggregated or anonymized personal data is therefore excluded from our privacy obligations. What else can we exclude from our "Personal Information" bucket?

First, if it's not about a person, it's not personal information. Maybe this sounds cheeky, but consider a hypothetical. Let's say a database contained information about my house. The color, the number windows it has, the types of flowers planted in the front yard. At first blush, this feels creepy. After all, this is my house—my "castle"—the place within which I have a federally protected right to privacy. Still, this data isn't about me: it's about my house. Without more, this is not personal information. We can thus exclude from this bucket data that may be sensitive but is not personal. Other examples of this may include a company's trade secrets, business plans, or marketing data.

What types of data should alert you to a potential privacy implication? Data about someone's race or ethnicity; religious beliefs; genetic and health data; sexual orientation; even military status and political opinions are protected in certain places. A good rule of thumb is to always be on the lookout for data that could be used for discriminatory purposes.

You get the idea. Protecting data about people is important. But assuming you aren't a privacy professional, how can you protect peoples' right to keep their private information out of the public domain? The rest of this section is designed to give you a framework for approaching personal data. This will help you understand whether to seek further advice from a privacy professional, and how to operationalize any privacy directives.

Generally accepted privacy principles

First helpful to understand are the Generally Accepted Privacy Principles, developed by the American Institute of Certified Public Accountants (AICPA) and the Canadian Institute of Charted Accountants (CICA) as a proposed global framework for privacy management. We will take just a few principles for an in-depth look. As you read these, please note that, while this is a proposed framework, many of these principles are codified in legislation like the GDPR.

QUICK
REFERENCE:

The 10 Generally Accepted Privacy Principles (GAPP)

1. **Management**—"the entity defines, documents, communicates, and assigns accountability for its privacy policies and procedures"

2. **Notice**—"the entity provides notice about its privacy policies and procedures and identifies the purposes for which personal information is collected, used, retained, and disclosed"

3. **Choice and Consent**—"the entity describes the choices available to the individual and obtains implicit or explicit consent with respect to the collection, use, and disclosure of personal information"

4. **Collection**—"the entity collects personal information only for the purposes identified in the notice and with…consent of the individual"

5. **Use, Retention, and Disposal**—"the entity retains personal information for only as long as necessary to fulfill the stated purposes or as required by law…"

6. **Access**—"the entity provides individuals with access to their personal information for review and update"

7. **Disclosure to Third Parties**—"the entity discloses personal information to third parties only for the purposes identified in the notice and with…consent of the individual"

8. **Security for Privacy**—"the entity protects personal information against unauthorized access"

9. **Quality**—"the entity maintains accurate, complete, and relevant personal information for the purposes identified in the notice"

10. **Monitoring and Enforcement**—"the entity monitors compliance with its privacy policies and procedures and has procedures to address privacy related inquiries, complaints, and disputes"

SOURCE: *General Accepted Privacy Principles (GAPP), American Institute of Certified Public Accountants (AICPA)*

What may have jumped out at you while reading the GAPP Principles is how multidisciplinary data privacy management is. That is, having someone to write policies and data protection agreements is not enough. Having someone to ensure the security of the systems holding sensitive data is not enough. Protecting private, personal information requires concerted action from legal professionals, security professionals, and data management professionals. Reading the GAPP list, do you have a sense about which items might fall, in whole or in part, on the data management team? I see seven out of the ten that, without a doubt, require at least some action from the data management team: management, choice and consent, collection, use, retention, and disposal, access, security and privacy, quality, and monitoring and enforcement. In truth, I could make an argument for all ten.

For precisely this reason, as a data leader, you should understand the principles of data privacy, even as the legal landscape continues to evolve. Because new privacy regulations are cropping up all the time, it would be impractical to list here every law you may be subject to.

That said, we can learn a lot from the categories of laws currently existing. Understanding the scope of laws covering personal data helps provide an intuition about when certain data under company management might require GAPP list activities. I've provided this overview from the vantage point of the American system, primarily because we are known for our complex patchwork of privacy laws. Countries outside the United States commonly have comprehensive, singular regulations. Following are examples of laws that indicate the breadth of data regulated.

Sectoral Laws

Sectoral laws are those data privacy laws that regulate a specific sector of the economy. When considering your company's privacy obligations, ask yourself if your company operates in, or handles data related to, one of these sectors:

- Communications, including social media (e.g., The Children's Online Privacy Protection Act (COPPA))
- Medical (e.g., The Health Insurance Portability and Accountability Act (HIPAA))
- Financial (e.g., Gramm-Leach-Bliley Act (GLBA))
- Education (e.g., Family Educational Rights and Privacy Act (FERPA))

State Laws

Your company could be subject to a state data privacy law

if it is headquartered or does business in the state. For example, if your company has an office in California, you may need to align your data management strategy with the following laws:

- California Financial Information Privacy Act (CFIPA)
- California Electronic Communications and Privacy Act (CalECPA)
- California Consumer Privacy Act (CCPA), as amended by California Privacy Rights Act (CPRA)

International Laws

Many companies today have a global presence. If your company is one of them, it could be subject to the privacy laws of each country in which it does business. Below are just a few examples of international privacy laws:

- The European Union's General Data Protection Regulation (GDPR)
- India's Digital Personal Data Protection Act (DPDP Act)
- China's Personal Information Protection Law (PIPL)
- Australia's Privacy Act and Australian Privacy Principles (APPs)
- Brazil's General Data Protection Law (LGPD)
- Tanzania's Personal Data Protection Act (PDPA)

Basics of a data privacy policy

It could be tempting to completely lock personal data up and allow not a soul to use it. But valid business reasons permit—and even require—use of personal data. How, then, do you balance access with privacy? For those categories of sensitive personal data discussed earlier, it is in your company's best interest to draft a policy detailing how this data can be accessed, by whom, in what circumstances, and for how long.

Such a policy can enact the ten GAPP principles, and it can

also support those who may be in the uncomfortable position of denying requests to access the sensitive data. A typical privacy policy will include provisions on data collection, retention, security, storage, use, and sharing. An example privacy policy is shown in Chapter 7.

To Be Secure: Data Security

We may think a data security lapse causes mainly reputational and financial damage to a business, but legal ramifications could also flow from some of the laws we just discussed. In addition to regulatory requirements, your company likely handles other sensitive business data that is subject to contractual obligations. Because of its importance to the business, your data team should work hand-in-hand with the security team to ensure security goals are upheld. Just as we did with the privacy laws, we will cover a few of the main principles of data security, as well as introduce concepts you will run into on your data journey.

Maintaining confidentiality, integrity, availability (CIA)

The main goals of data security are succinctly monikered "CIA": confidentiality; integrity; and availability. We are likely familiar with the concept of confidentiality; in a security environment, ensuring unauthorized individuals cannot access sensitive data is a keystone priority. Those of us outside the security profession might not know that good data security also protects systems and data from unauthorized changes (integrity) and unexpected downtime (availability).

As one of the main data stewards for your company, you play an integral role in safeguarding private and closely held data.

If you own key company databases, you are likely responsible for minimizing risks and vulnerabilities through proper system maintenance like updates and patches. But you will also need to consider how to keep the data confidential through encryption, obfuscation, masking, or aggregation (refer to "Quick Reference: Security Terms Decoder").

Quick Reference:

Security Terms Decoder

Vulnerability—A weakness or defect in a system that allows it to be successfully attacked and compromised. Examples include out-of-date security patches or weak passwords.

Risk— Both the possibility of loss and the thing or condition that poses potential loss.

Encryption—The process of translating plain text into complex codes to hide privileged information, verify complete transmission, or verify the sender's identity. Examples include hash, symmetric, private-key, and public-key encryption.

Obfuscation and Masking—Making the data unreadable or unclear by removing, shuffling, or otherwise changing the appearance of data without losing the meaning of the data or the relationships the data has to other data sets, such as foreign key relationships. Examples include substitution, randomization, encryption, nulling or deleting.

> SOURCE: *DAMA-DMBOK*

Creating an access program

Finally, work with your security team to create a role-based access program for the company's sensitive data. They will likely have already designed a classification system where information is designated as either confidential, restricted, internal, or public. Which roles in the company can access the data in each of those classification layers? It may not be immediately feasible to automate this role-based access, but you can greatly reduce confusion and misapplication of the standards if you establish a repeatable process early on.

To Be Fair: Data Ethics

Often privacy and security are given the most attention because legal and reputational penalties can be severe. Indeed, even I started this chapter with a love-letter (of sorts) to privacy law. But the ethical handling of data is just as important if you are to have a successful data program. This is because "ethical" in this scenario doesn't mean that we're good people. It means that we've established practices that reduce or eliminate the potential for skewed, inaccurate, or misleading outcomes. Further, because AI and technology development continues to accelerate at rates faster than we can regulate, I predict that data ethics will be our main source of harm prevention and accountability into the foreseeable future. Ethical data handling thus has both a business and a societal benefit.

For the purposes of our discussion here, I am going to side-step the purposeful mishandling of data and focus just on the pitfalls in which we might find ourselves if we aren't careful. With that caveat, we can largely divide unethical data handling into two groups: fallacies and biases. Because they are similar—especially in the untrustworthy outcomes they generate—fallacies and biases are often lumped together with respect to data. But I want to distinguish the two. A slight, but fundamental, difference exists between a fallacy and a bias. A bias occurs at the time of data collection or analysis, while a fallacy occurs at the time of interpretation or presentation.

Fallacies

If you resonated with the "bridge logic" example from the first chapter, you are already familiar with fallacies. Simply put, a fallacy is a defect in reasoning we use to support an argument. Like the straw man fallacy evident in the bridge example, other logical fallacies can also befall our data interpretation. Let's discuss two of the most prevalent.

Hasty generalizations

First is the *Hasty Generalization*. We've all done this: jumped to a conclusion before we had sufficient evidence, or made a decision based on evidence that perhaps wasn't so reliable. Let's check back in with our moms for a classic example: you're five years old and your mom has made Brussels sprouts for dinner. "I don't like that," you say, raising an eyebrow at the odd thing placed on your dinner plate. "Have you ever tried one?" she asks. Dang—she's got you there. But you didn't jump to your conclusion out of sheer obstinate desire. Based on the evidence in front of you, you're sure you aren't going to like that tiny cabbage. First of all, it smells weird. Second of all, it just doesn't look like something that should be on your plate, right? But, in this instance, your mom has the better of the logic. You cannot know that you don't like the taste of Brussels sprouts until you taste one.

Happy Data

QUICK
REFERENCE:

Hasty Generalization[29] (aka Survivorship Bias): A conclusion based on insufficient or biased evidence.

How does this phenomenon show up in our data? Let's take another classic example: the story of Abraham Wald and The Missing Bullet Holes.[30] During World War II, the United States military sought the help of a group of mathematicians from Columbia University with a seemingly-straightforward—albeit high-stakes—optimization problem. The more armor they added to their fighter pilots' planes, reasoned the military, the more protected its pilots would be from artillery (bullets). But armoring the entire plane would be impractical because more armor means a heavier and more expensive plane. Hence, the military's request to Abraham Wald and his team of statisticians: find the amount of armor we can put on our planes to balance safety and function.

The military gave Wald some data they had collected from planes that had returned home from Europe. These planes had come back riddled with bullet holes. But the holes weren't equally distributed across the planes as one might expect. They were largely concentrated on the fuselage and the extremities of the plane—rarely on the engine. A-ha! That must be the answer, then. Simply put more armor around the fuselage and wings. Indeed, that was the assumed solution the military had brought to Wald. But Wald challenged this assumption. Statistically speaking, the bullet holes should be evenly distributed. So, what did the lack of uniformity mean?

The military only had bullet data on the planes that came back. If they didn't see bullet holes on the engines of the planes that returned home, it's because planes that got shot in the engines didn't return home. The vulnerable part of the plane isn't the fuselage: it's the engine. That's where your armor goes.

These two examples of hasty generalizations are wildly different, but they have something in common. Notice that in neither example did we make a decision based on no data. Notice that we didn't even make a decision based on bad data. This type of fallacy happens when we make a decision without having the full picture. To guard against this, ask: what assumptions have I made? What data might I be missing? Of course, asking you to know what you don't know might be unhelpful; don't be afraid to take a page out of the military's play book and seek out a second set of eyes.

Post hoc ergo propter hoc

The second fallacy we see frequently in the data world is what logicians call "Post hoc ergo propter hoc" ("after this, therefore, because of this"). Data people usually just say that "correlation does not imply causation."

QUICK REFERENCE:

Post hoc ergo propter hoc[31] **(aka False Causality)** — A conclusion that assumes that if event 'A' occurs before or together with event 'B,' then 'A' must be the cause of 'B.'

If you have never treated yourself to Tyler Vigen's *Spurious Correlations* website,[32] put that on your to-do list. Vigen's project exploits the fact that two wildly unrelated events can correlate almost perfectly. Take his example in Figure 15 showing the number of associates degrees in math and statistics correlating almost perfectly with the rate of Google searches for "dollar store near me."

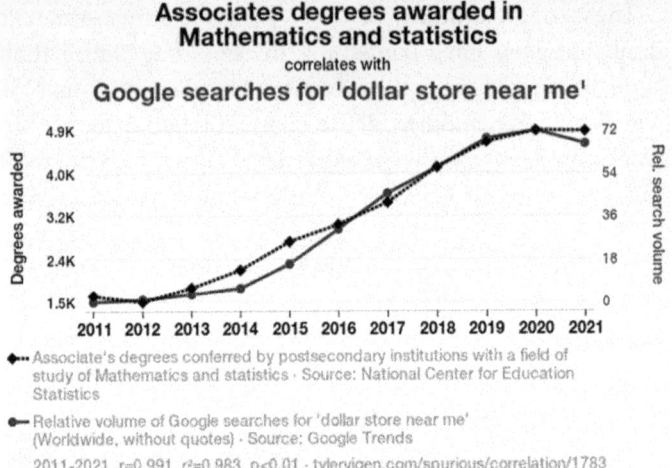

Figure 15

You are a smart person, and I'll bet you could rationalize a causal relationship between these two events. Maybe a job for someone with a degree in math and statistics doesn't pay well, so people with those degrees have to shop at the dollar store? Plausible, but unlikely given the average salary of an entry-level statistician is nearly $70,000[33] and people of all income levels shop at dollar stores.

Artificial Intelligence is also smart (it says so right in the name); maybe it can better explain a causal relationship between these two events. Here is AI's best effort: [34]

> "As the number of Associates degrees awarded in Mathematics and statistics goes up, so does the nation's love for all things numerical. This newfound passion for counting leads people to realize that dollar stores are not only economical but also prime spots for mathematical calculations. From calculating the best

deals to budgeting for their next shopping spree, it all adds up to a surge in interest for dollar stores. So, the next time you're searching for a dollar store near you, just remember, it's not just about the savings, it's about the mathemagical experience that awaits!"

Colorful, but this still feels off the mark. While all of the examples on Vigen's website are extreme, his point is clear: just because two or more events look related doesn't necessarily mean they have any bearing on each other in reality. And if you and I and AI could come up with plausible explanations for the dollar store correlation, we could be even more convincing with data that is not so obviously unrelated.

Luckily, we have straightforward methods to guard against this type of fallacy. First, we should always define the precise question we seek to answer before we start analyzing data. In other words, it is unethical to look at a trove of data and start mining it to see if you can uncover any interesting relationships. This is called "data dredging." It has no place in data analysis.

Second, we should always ask whether a third factor that we haven't yet considered could have caused both of the events. In our example above, perhaps the founder of everyone's favorite dollar store is a new investor on Shark Tank, and he always talks about how his associate's degree in mathematics and statistics helped him launch his billion-dollar entrepreneurial enterprise. Having a nationally televised platform, he inspires people across the country to get a similar degree and to check out their local dollar store.

The second method is undoubtedly harder to work. But you don't have to actually find the alternate explanation to have handled the problem ethically. All you have to do, assuming other factors are not clear in the data, is to say in your reporting that other factors may have contributed to the result (or the strength of the result), but you had insufficient data to explore them.

Biases

When we taste tiny portions of ice cream in tiny spoons, we feel confident in basing our final ice cream order on those tiny tests. Why? We see the worker behind the counter scoop directly from the giant barrel of our chosen flavor, and, because each flavor gets its own barrel, we are comfortable that the flavor will be the same regardless of where it's scraped from. But what if each flavor didn't get its own barrel? What if dozens of flavors were randomly peppered throughout one mega-barrel?

Unless you and the worker devised an incisive tiny-scoop extraction plan, you would probably be less confident that your final order would taste the same as your sample. But let's say the situation was even more dire. Let's say a worker from the previous shift thought it would be fun to swirl all of the ice cream together throughout our already precarious trough? Now, depending on where we stick that tiny spoon, we could taste a range of flavors that wouldn't reveal themselves until we took the first bite. How can we make a reliable ordering decision now?

If you're like me, you'd probably ask the poor worker to stick a few tiny spoons randomly throughout the ice cream trough. A few random samples would probably give you a decent idea of what your final order will taste like, right?

Well, statistically speaking, that is a great route to take (though it might not do much for your interpersonal relationship with the worker). Because of the lack of uniformity, a single sample from a spot that looks to you like mostly vanilla might taste quite different from the final product. In other words: that sample is biased.

It turns out life is a lot like that vat of swirled ice cream. When analyzing real-world phenomena, then, we must apply similar sampling techniques to ensure any generalization we make to a broader population is unbiased — that is, that we aren't setting ourselves up to rely on an incorrect inference. We can guard against this sampling bias in two ways: by ensuring our sample is both random and the right size.

INSIGHT:

Inferential Statistics

There are two types of statistics: (1) descriptive statistics and (2) inferential statistics. Descriptive statistics describe a complete set of data. Inferential statistics look only at a sample to make a conclusion about the population. For example, let's say you survey 200 employees on their preferences for remote work, and use their responses to infer that the whole company would, on average, respond the same way. The 200 employees would be your sample, and you would draw a conclusion about the whole company (the population).

Getting an appropriate sample size

A sample describes a part of the population from which data is collected. The population is the whole group being studied. In selecting a sample, ask: who do we want to be able to generalize our results to? Are we interested in everyone in the company? A single department? All companies in the same industry throughout the world?

Luckily, several online calculators exist that can help you determine the appropriate sample size for your analysis (see the Selected Resources section of Chapter 7).

Making sure the sample is random

Ensuring a truly random sample is undoubtedly trickier

and, indeed, we could take up half of this book discussing sampling methods. But a good guideline here is to simply ask yourself: in my data collection, is one group of people more likely to participate (in other words: provide data) than others? If so, can you increase the chances that people in other groups participate? For example, could you randomly select email addresses to send your survey to?

Of course, our overarching goal is to gather data that we can rely on to make decisions. But sometimes, we just can't get an ideal sample. We can still maintain ethical data handling practices by noting our sample sizes, assumptions, and available generalizations in our reports.

Cherry picking

The second bias we need to talk about requires little explanation. We have all experienced it in wild internet arguments or fights with friends. Many of us have probably even done it ourselves. I'm talking about cherry picking. If you select results that support your argument and ignore those that don't, you're cherry picking. If I want to persuade my firm's leaders to fund another year of my data literacy program based on the claim that firm employees love the content, I can't show them ten positive reviews and withhold thirty negative ones.

Fortunately, you can guard against cherry-picked data using methods we've already discussed. If you are the one doing the analysis, define the question you want to answer ahead of time (e.g., what are my colleagues' perceptions about my data literacy content?). If you are on the receiving end of the data, ask what, if any, data was excluded from analysis.

Biases and fallacies undermine both the soundness of decisions and the credibility of any argument you make based on data. Ethical data handling is thus critical to a successful business. I encourage you to bake in this third layer of protection—along with privacy and security—to your data handling practices.

CHAPTER FOUR
Gilligan's Data

"How can we ensure our data aren't islands unto themselves?" That's the thought I wondered aloud in a conversation with my team about addressing silos early on in our data journey. As it often happens, the discussion digressed as we congratulated ourselves for pinpointing "people stranded on a deserted island" as a better metaphor than "silos."

I prefer the "island" metaphor because it frames the problem, not as a fight to extract data from quarantine, but as a mission to help people and data connect. Framing the problem in this way allows us to ask more helpful questions like, "How can we bring people together to solve issues?" "How can we make it simpler for data to travel across systems?" "How can we connect people to their place in the company's overall value proposition?" This simple mindset shift elevates data as an asset owned by the business, rather than by individual departments, and spurs activities to promote connection to data, to each other, and to a purpose. By reading this chapter and completing the prompts, you are able to:

- ✓ Understand how to leverage the IKEA Effect for sustainable outcomes
- ✓ Craft your own issue management plan
- ✓ Begin a conceptual data model for your organization
- ✓ Understand how data virtualization physically and culturally dissolves silos

A Camel Walks into IKEA...

In 2011, researchers Michael Norton, Daniel Mochon, and Dan Ariely asked a question. How can Build-a-Bear charge more than double the price of an average teddy bear while passing the burden of assembly on to consumers? As a child in the 1990s, I can attest to the success of the Build-a-Bear business model. For years there wasn't a single Saturday where the line at Build-a-Bear wasn't snaking outside its own mall storefront—and across the entrances of several others. Was it fun using a giant machine to blow stuffing into a lifeless Hello Kitty skin? Sure. But it turns out the thrill of the experience alone doesn't explain why Do-It-Yourself products are so popular.

In *The "IKEA Effect": When Labor Leads to Love*, Norton and his colleagues (collectively "Norton") describe a series of experiments showing that people will place more value on a product if they build themselves. In the first experiment, Norton gives half the participants an unassembled box with assembly instructions from IKEA and the other half a pre-assembled version of the same box. The first half were told to assemble their boxes, and then both sets of participants were asked to inspect their boxes. After inspection, Norton asked participants to (1) rate how much, on a 7-point scale, they liked their boxes, and (2) say how much they would be willing to pay for their box. Not only did builders like their boxes better than non-builders, they also offered to buy their boxes for prices, on average, 60 percent higher.

As further proof that value is not intrinsic to a good, but rather something we assign to it, Norton's experiments also show that people will not overvalue a project if they either do not complete it or if they disassemble it after completion. Norton's findings aren't a mere novelty. They demonstrate our human desire to feel useful and effective. This "IKEA Effect" can pose problems in a corporate setting if it causes us to forgo a superior product because "it wasn't invented here." But we can use the psychological underpinnings of the Effect to drive collaborative projects to a successful end.

Bubbling just beneath the surface of every breathless business consultant begging us to dismantle a silo is an implicit reference to the IKEA Effect. If we invite our colleagues to help us create our processes, they will place a higher value on the outcomes than if we handed down mandates from on-high. Our beleaguered consultant knows this. Logically, we know it too. Yet, we walk a perpetual tightrope between authority and facilitator.

It's almost a truism at this point to say that siloed teams lead to siloed data. Yes, we all get it: silos belong on barns, not in boardrooms. But it's one thing to say you're going to collaborate and bust those corporate silos. It's another thing to identify the opportunities to do that in practice. Besides, you don't want to mire every one of your activities down in bureaucracy. Some things you'll decide alone. Silos get a bad rap, but often committees are just as vilified. People are on record as far back as the 1950s deriding the products of group work.[35] "A camel," the adage goes, "is a horse designed by committee." Of course, this isn't really fair to camels. They're useful beasts of burden, especially when crossing arid landscapes. You don't want a horse for your trek across the Sahara; you want an animal that carries its own water.

The real question you need to ask yourself, then, is not

whether a committee is less useless than a silo. Rather, ask yourself: for this trip, do I need a horse, or do I need a camel? Does the legitimacy of this project depend on the number and variety of people that gave input? Or can the business rely on my expertise for this decision? A good rule of thumb is that if an activity is meant to improve or benefit your own team, do it alone. If it's meant to confer value to the company, do it together. But you know I'm not going to leave you with a rule of thumb. So let's walk through specific activities where you can safely leave your horse behind and walk that camel confidently into the closest IKEA.

The Issue Management Process

Issues arise as part of the data governance process and may take various forms: differing positions on the application of an existing policy, discovery of a data quality issue, or proposals for standard contract terms regarding data handling, just to name a few. Creating a reliable process for resolving these myriad issues not only saves your sanity—it proves the value and credibility of your team.

However the organization manages its data mirrors its broader processes for managing issues. If data is managed ad hoc and largely within silos, issues are also likely dispensed of within those silos. When it comes to data, we want to centralize that issue management process as much as is practical within the operating model we've chosen. This means that if you've set up a data governance board, council, and steward apparatus, issue management will flow through this hierarchy. If you don't have this hierarchy yet: don't worry. The goal here is to center issue management around the data, not the department. This enables consistent, dependable, and traceable results.

Whether formalized or not, ad hoc or not, four major

activities define the issue management process. The process is roughly cyclical as we triage, document, communicate, and resolve issues (see Figure 16). I say "roughly" cyclical because you might (and, often, should) find yourself pinging back and forth between activities before exiting the cycle. We don't want to save our communication with stakeholders until we reach a final decision; we want to communicate with them throughout the process. We want to document at each phase of the process so that we have a complete record of how we reached a decision. We may exit the cycle after the Resolve activities—or we may find that our solution misses the mark somewhere. In that case, we will need to start Triage again.

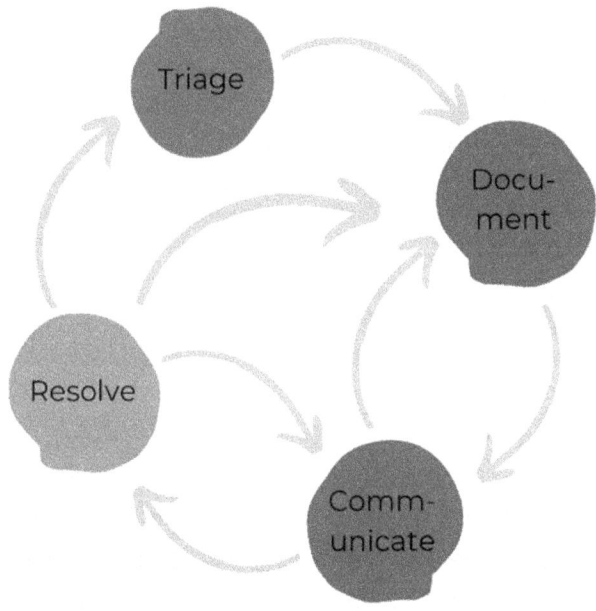

Figure 16

Triage

In Triage, we need to understand two key questions: (1) have we seen this problem before and (2) what type of issue is it? At the outset, we need to know whether this issue is new or known because we shouldn't start from scratch if we don't need to. We also need to know, if the issue is recurrent, what we've already tried that hasn't worked. If the issue is new, we then need to categorize it. The issue category will help us prioritize the urgent and consult appropriate subject matter experts. The DAMA-DMBOK calls out eight distinct issue categories:[36]

- **Authority:** questions or issues related to decision rights and procedures
- **Change:** issues arising from a change management process
- **Compliance:** problems meeting compliance requirements
- **Conflicts:** conflicting policies, procedures, business rules, names, definitions, standards, architecture, and interests
- **Conformance:** issues with a lack of conformance to policies, standards, architecture, and procedures
- **Contracts:** negotiation and review of data-related contracts, like data sharing agreements
- **Security:** privacy and confidentiality issues
- **Quality:** identification and resolution of data quality issues

Document

Documenting the issue—and your activities throughout the issue management process—is a vital step to ensuring a smooth and lasting resolution. Sadly, I am a horrible note-taker. I mean really awful. I have sticky-notes and loose pieces of paper scattered across my desk; I hardly fare better in a digital environment. My approach to notetaking is not good enough if I want to create a transparent and reliable issue record. Knowing my weakness, I created an issue record template in Microsoft

Word. The template, shown in Figures 17 and 18, ensures I and others on my team follow our own process and preserve necessary information to take an issue from intake to resolution. The repeatable sections in this form allow us to add notes specific to each phase.

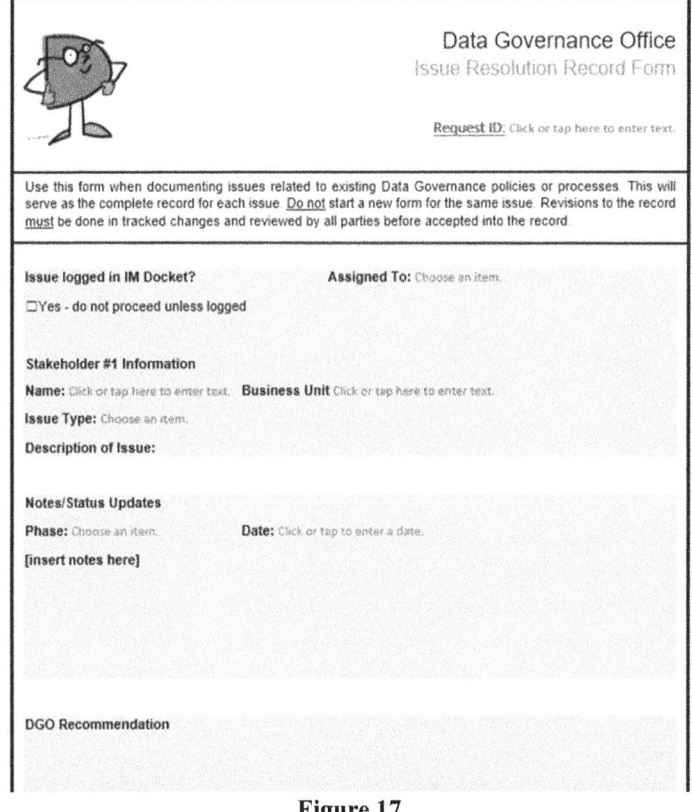

Figure 17
(To download a free copy of this template, visit happydatacompany.com/resources)

My team's issue management process begins with fact-finding where we learn about the genesis of the issue. The process may then go through a chain of authorities—our data stewards, data governance council, and data governance board—until we agree to a remediation plan. We keep any other documentation relating to project scope, requirements, code, policies, or standards separate from this issue record. Once the issue is resolved, we enter any closing notes and use the record to certify that we've completed all parts of the process.

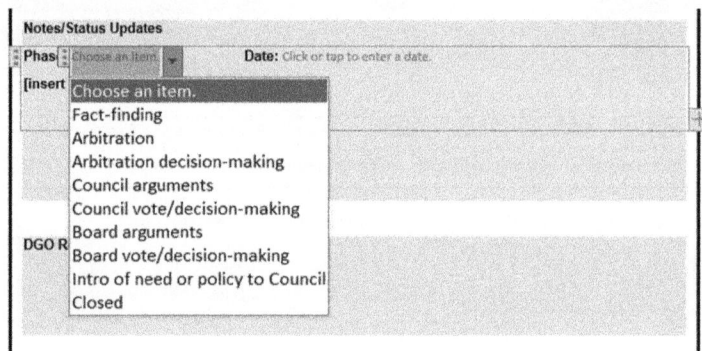

Figure 18

How you manage and store all this issue management collateral is largely a matter of preference, but I recommend keeping everything in a centralized location. If you have a data catalog, you could take advantage of its built-in workflows. If not, set up an issue intake form. If you have Microsoft Office or Google Suite, you can use their Forms functionality. If you don't have any Forms functionality, set up an email inbox where your colleagues can send their issues. You can keep all of these records together in any shared folder, intranet, or document management system. This goal here is to make these records publicly available so that others can rely on the decisions going forward.

Communicate

This record template assumes—and, indeed, requires—that

you communicate with relevant stakeholders throughout the process. But don't neglect to communicate the outcome; often a broader group will have an interest in the decision than just the original group of stakeholders. For example, let's say you were working through a data quality issue, and the data governance council decided to implement a policy requiring a standard format for data entry. People throughout the organization will need to know, at a minimum, what the format is and that it is required.

That final communication to your broader organization, like the example in Figure 19, can be simple. Providing the date, scope, and important restrictions in a notice that you distribute via email or post in your data catalog or company intranet is sufficient.

DATA GOVERNANCE
COUNCIL RESOLUTION
MEMORANDUM FOR RECORD

Effective Date: 1 September 2022

Decision to Provide Billing Data to CRM System

At the data governance council meeting held September 1, 2022, the marketing team presented their request to gather certain financial data for use in a customer relationship management system. Council approved the request and agreed on the usage guidelines below.

SCOPE

The marketing team requests access to select billing data to upload to the company's CRM system. CRM is a cloud-based service that provides various marketing-related functionality, including tracking client activity and engagement. Marketing requests the following data:

- Billed Amount
- Billed Date
- Billed Minutes
- Timestamp
- Work Date
- Worked Minutes

DECISION OF COUNCIL

- RESOLVED that the billing data described above may be provided to the marketing team for upload into the CRM for the purpose of tracking client activity and engagement.
- RESOLVED that the source of the data detailed above will be designated by the finance team.
- RESOLVED that such data will be subject to filters and masks as specified by the risk management team. Masking may including substituting an actual name for a generic label (e.g., "CONFIDENTIAL" or "********").

Figure 19
(To download a free copy of this template, visit

happydatacompany.com/resources)

Resolve

Once you intake and triage the issue, you are ready to enter the Resolve phase. The resolution process starts with the data governance council, who follow a process for determining steps to address the issue and include, if necessary, mechanisms (such as informal arbitration) for addressing disputes and disagreements between parties.

Deep Dive: Data Governance Issue Management Process

While the activities depicted in Figure 16 are (or should be) present in any issue management process, the procedure your team uses to engage with stakeholders and resolve issues could vary depending on your operating model. You have already seen a rough sketch of the issue management process I've employed in my work, but let's now view that process more in depth and focus on the steps a single issue goes through on its way to resolution.

Step 1: Issue Triage and Fact-finding

The first act is understanding if the issue is novel or whether it relates to an existing standard, policy, or process. By "existing standard, policy, or process," I mean an action the data governance team has implemented in response to a known issue. If the issue relates to an existing standard, policy, or process, then the data governance team reaches out to the issue submitter to learn more and develop a remediation plan. If the issue is new or data governance has not yet implemented a standard, policy, or process to address an issue, the issue is placed on the agenda for the next data governance council meeting. We then categorize the issue (see the "Triage" section of this chapter) and begin the fact-finding phase. We encourage all our data stewards, council members, board members, and working group members to input their issue into our centralized data catalog. This allows the data governance team to efficiently track and update the issue.

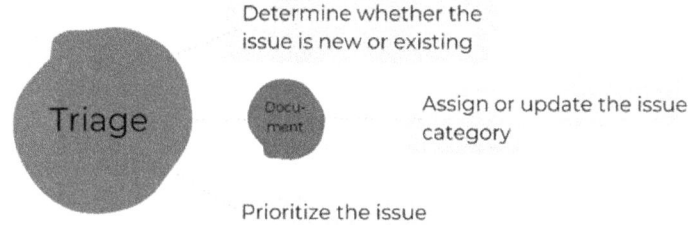

Figure 20

Step 2: Arbitration

After data governance has implemented a policy, standard, or process, questions may arise regarding if or how the policy, standard, or process should apply. Whatever the cause, issues related to an existing data governance policy, standard, or process will submit to arbitration among the disputing parties. The arbitration process (Figure 21) is meant to resolve issues at the data steward level. This process does not apply if an issue has reached the council or board levels.

Gilligan's Data

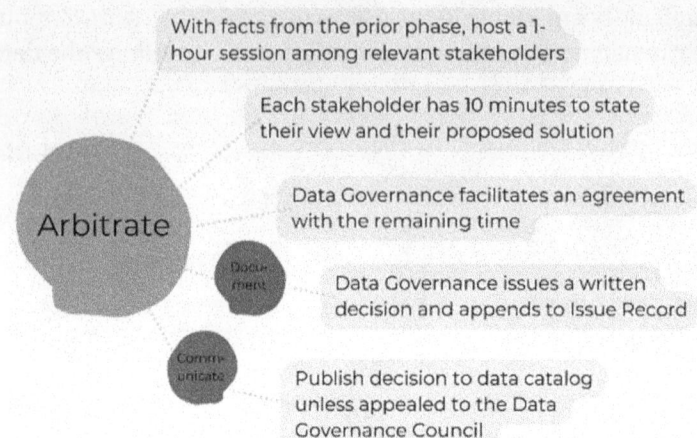

Figure 21

Step 3: Appeal to Council

Any party involved in the arbitration process may request to appeal the data governance team's decision to the data governance council. Parties must request an appeal within five business days of the data governance team's written decision. During Appeal (Figure 22), data governance presents the issue, findings, arguments from all sides, and the decision from the Arbitration phase. Ten minutes are allotted for this unless a time extension is granted. The council has 15 minutes to deliberate. Data governance then asks if the council is ready to vote. If not, additional deliberation time is scheduled for the next council meeting.

If council needs more time, ask how long they need to deliberate and whether the issue is big enough to create a working group. If the council is ready to vote at the end of the deliberation period, data governance goes around the "table" and asks each member which solution they vote for. Council can either accept data governance's prior decision, one of the other arguments, a new solution, or a combination of all three. If 75 percent of the participating council agree to the solution, data governance documents the solution and sends it to the council to review and approve. Data governance publishes the solution to the appropriate forum, communicates the decision to the original parties, and closes the issue. If the council is unable to reach a conclusion, the issue escalates to the data governance board.

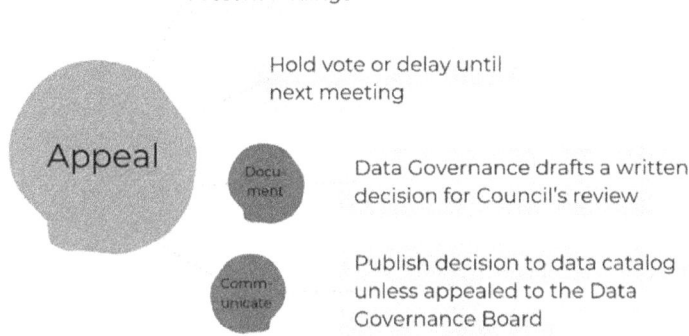

Figure 22

Step 4: Appeal to Board

In the case that 75 percent of participating council members do not reach an agreement as to the reading of a policy or resolution of an issue, the issue escalates to the data governance board. In the board appeal process (Figure 23), data governance presents the findings and conclusions from below and reminds the board of their options for issue resolution. They may choose to uphold the decision from below; overturn the decision from below and provide an alternate solution; or issue guidance and remand to the council for a new solution according to the guidance. After data governance presents the issue, they ask if the board is ready to vote on a resolution. If not, deliberations extend through emails or other meetings. If the issue is big enough, data governance creates a working group. If the board is ready to vote at the end of the deliberation period, data governance goes around the "table" and each member votes for a solution. If 75 percent of the participating board members agree to the solution, data governance documents the solution and sends it to the board to review and approve. Data governance publishes the solution to the appropriate forum, communicates to the original parties, and closes the issue. If the board chooses to issue guidance and remand to the council, return to Step 3: Appeal to council.

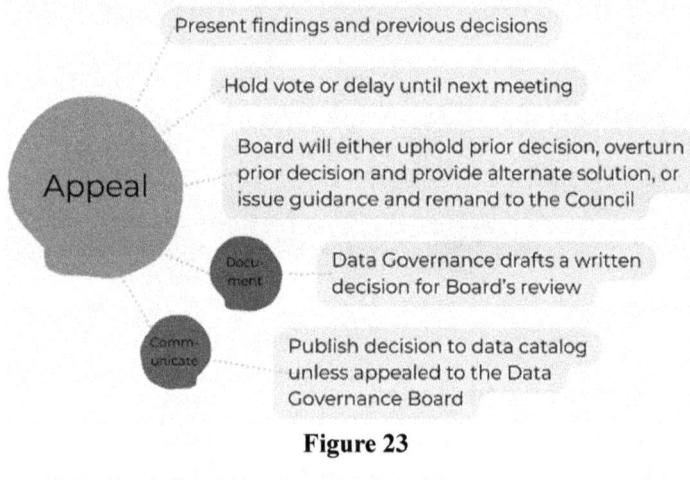

Figure 23

Model Citizen

If you had to describe how your business worked in five sentences or less to someone who had no prior knowledge of the industry, how would you do it? If you owned a bookstore, you might say:

I buy books from agencies and independent authors at wholesale prices, put them on the shelves of my store, and sell them to customers at retail price.

If you ran a lawn care business, you might say:

Homeowners pay me to help them develop and implement a lawn maintenance or improvement plan. I have a team of people who specialize in various aspects of landscaping. Depending on the needs of the homeowner, they hire my team to do a one-time job or to come back at regular intervals.

Generating a high-level model of your business

Of course, the inner workings of any business are much more complex than five sentences. We have to manage vendors and pay taxes; handle pay roll and market our products. Why should we shove ourselves into a five-sentence box? Well, let me ask a different question. What do the people throughout your organization agree on? If you're just starting your data management journey, you most likely responded to my question one of two ways. You either said "not much" or you shrugged because you just don't know yet.

Regardless of your answer, regardless of your current state, I can see into your future. If your colleagues haven't disagreed about data yet, they will. It's going to be your job to get them to come together. That's a hard job. But it will go from hard to impossible if people don't first agree to the most basic things: what business you're in, who your customers are, and how you make money. These major axis points are the foundation from which all of your data and processes flow. Generating a high-level model of your business like this thus serves both business and technical goals. It serves business goals because it acts as a jumping off point for intricate decisions, and it serves technical goals because it helps you define your main data domains.

Understanding data domains

What's a data domain? Depends on who you ask. You'll find broad agreement that a domain is the biggest bucket you can put categories of data in. A domain that most businesses will have is a "customers" domain (or, if you're in professional services, you might have a "clients" domain). You probably have a few different categories of customer data—customer demographic data, customer transaction history, and so on. But at the highest level of abstraction, we can tie all of these different categories together under one "customers" domain, creating an explicit hierarchy that serves metadata management, governance, and architectural goals.

Good versus bad domains

What people less frequently agree on is what makes for a good domain. I have seen domains that fall along a company's lines of business—for example, a bank's lines of business might be consumer banking, commercial banking, credit, and loans. If in Chapter 3 you thought your organization would benefit from a decentralized governance structure, this approach to domains might be a good fit.

The other way I have seen companies implement domains is by department. That is, they will have a human resources domain, a marketing domain, a finance domain, and so on. These, I think, are unhelpful distinctions. First, they further solidify the silos we are trying to tear down. They reinforce the narrative that HR "owns" its data, that Finance "owns" its data.

Remember: data doesn't belong to any one department: it belongs to the company.

Second, while it may seem like breaking data down by department provides granularity, this approach is overly blunt. Let me explain. Some data fields are wholly specific to a department and as such are rarely touched by other teams. An example of this may be the payroll company codes that exist in your payroll system and determine which entity an employee's salary is drawn from. This is a transactional data point that is unlikely to find its way into any company-wide analytics—and, even if it did, there's no room for gray area in the definition of a payroll company code.

Many—if not most—of the data you will care about, however, is that data that is used by multiple departments. One piece of data may serve several purposes and have just as many incarnations. Take the term "Full Time Equivalent (FTE)." If a person works a full-time schedule, their FTE is 1; a person working part-time would have an FTE less than 1 but greater than 0. This concept has scheduling implications, which we might consider an HR issue. But it also has financial implications: we have to, of course, pay employees equal to their time worked, and we also have to factor in the various FTEs into our annual hiring budgets. Were we to shove the FTE term into an HR domain alone, we would neglect the nuance that our data consumers need to understand this data.

As the FTE example shows, not every field of data will fit neatly into a domain, just like your five-sentence description won't perfectly describe your business. What you're doing here is creating a model that explains the typical scenario. When you create a model, you aren't concerned with describing reality perfectly. You should thus try to avoid getting ensnared in edge cases and instead rely on the maxim that "all models are wrong, but some are useful."

A professional services example

Let's see how this works using my five-sentence-or-less description of a typical law firm business model.

> *As a full-service international law firm, we (the primary organization) hire legal and business services professionals (our people) to work on matters for clients. Not all people will*

interact with clients or work on matters, as certain business professionals perform work for the law firm as a whole (e.g., the firm's finance or technology teams). The main organization is made up of smaller organizations called practice groups, subgroups, departments, and teams. Likewise, clients can comprise several related clients and matters can comprise related matters. Organization, Client, Person, and Matter are thus the four major domains that categorize all of the firm's data.

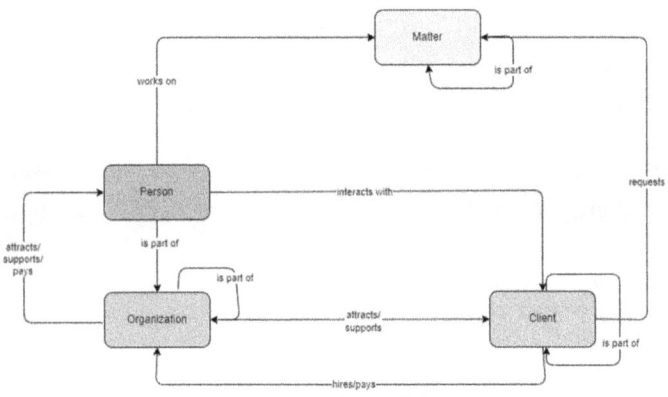

Figure 24

In Figure 24, each domain is related to another, creating a graphical representation of my 5-sentence business description. With this, I have begun a conceptual data model for my organization. Notice how I can grab one of the four domains, Person, and expand it out to show all attributes that might describe that domain (Figure 25). You can see in Figure 25 that a Person is classified by a Person Type (e.g., a lawyer or business professional), they have a compensation structure and a schedule structure, they may work on matters and report to a supervisor, they sit in a physical office location and are assigned to a particular organization (practice group or department).

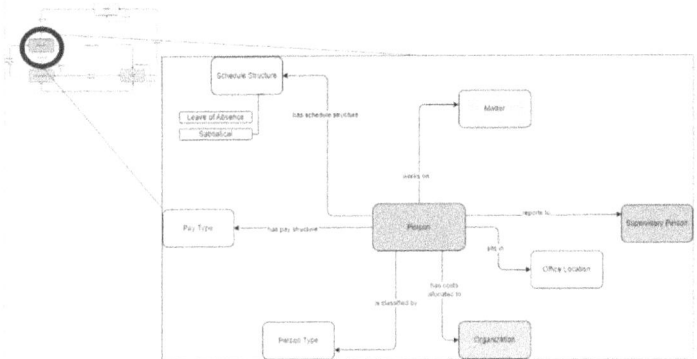

Figure 25

If needed, we can break these attributes down even further conceptually. Or, if we can't break concepts down further, this signals that we've reached a point of being able to attach the physical data to the concept (Figure 26).

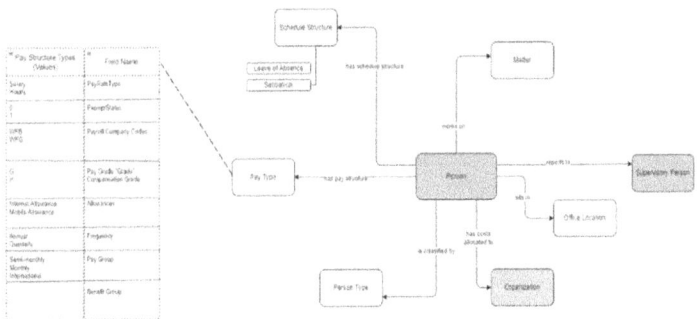

Figure 26

Developing a conceptual data model

While it may seem academic or theoretical, I am a big fan of developing a conceptual data model with your council. At the highest level, modeling lays the groundwork for future problem-solving as discussed a moment ago. But it's also a power tool for your Organizational Archeology. You can dig, layer by layer, from domain to concept to category to data field, defining and documenting important metadata as you go.

I created my first conceptual data model for a couple of reasons. First, my data governance council was finding it hard to give feedback and agree on definitions for our business terms. I can't blame them. Simply given the word "Practice" without any context, I wouldn't know how to define it either. Second, we had been given a general direction to "fix" our "people data." There was just one problem: nobody really knew what the universe of "people data" was that we'd need to consider. What were all of the fields? What were they used for? Who used them? What other processes did they feed? And, since they apparently needed "fixed," what was wrong with them? Without the conceptual model, answering these questions was like wading through a giant ball pit in search of one specific ball. We didn't really know where to start, and it was hard to tell where we'd been.

But as we went along, we found that the model provided a lot of other benefits as well. Just the act of creating the model helped us understand where the work of our departments intersects and where we have gaps in data or processes. It also allowed us to develop a full taxonomy of our business data for our data catalog. Now, anyone in the firm can come browse data in the catalog at increasing levels of detail. This additional context helps analysts know which data is the right data for their analysis, where previously they might have grabbed at the nearest database and cajoled whatever data was within their reach.

The other benefit to creating this council-approved conceptual model is that it gives us a basis to manage exceptions and constrain future architecture decisions. That is, we can more easily see what the typical set of values is for a concept or a field and consciously decide whether a deviation will be worth the ding to data quality. This is not to say there will never be an exception—or even that the model will perfectly capture the full state of your data environment and its approved exceptions. Remember, we're not going for perfection here. We're going for useful.

From Spaghetti to the Benefits of Data Virtualization

I promised I wouldn't get too technical in this book, but a third opportunity to bust silos is too good to pass up. In the data space, we face a common architectural pattern called a "spaghetti" architecture. The spaghetti architecture got its name because when all point-to-point data integrations within a company are diagrammed it looks like a bowl of spaghetti (see the example in Figure 27).

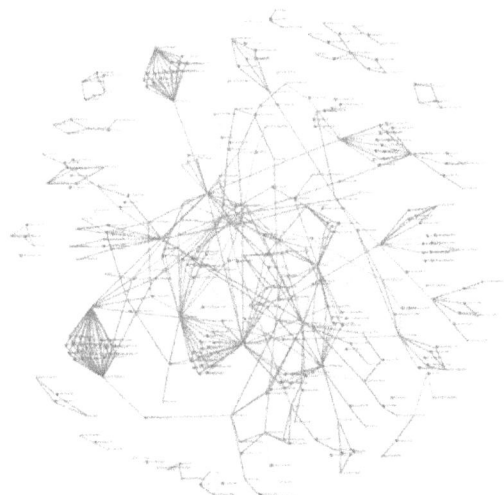

Figure 27
Image description: each point represents a technology product. Each line represents an integration from that system to another.

All of these point-to-point integrations are expensive and difficult to maintain, which is why many of the top technology companies like Meta and Netflix opt to virtualize their data instead. With virtualization, we are not connecting each data source to each other, nor are we storing physical copies of the data in a central repository. Instead, we create a central access, or viewing, layer for data from any source system. If, for example, the finance team needs to run a report that also uses data from HR, they would no longer need to physically connect the finance and HR systems. Instead, they could connect to that centralized virtual layer. In this way, we can move away from the cumbersome spaghetti architecture and toward a hub-and-spoke pattern (Figure 28).

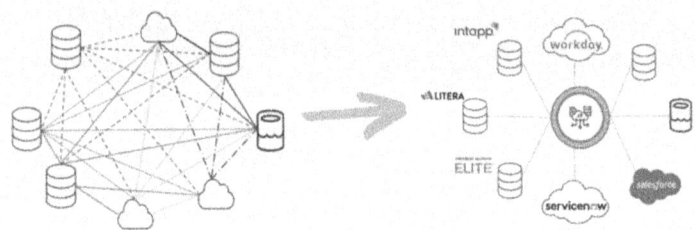

Figure 28

Managing technology costs is just one benefit of data virtualization, as it also provides unified security and governance. But that's not really what this chapter is about. This chapter is about getting data off individual islands so it can be used for the greater good. Data virtualization is one of the few ways we can physically break down our silos, as the distribution of the data itself disintegrates the walls that previously kept it inaccessible.

Virtualization is also an opportunity to become better collaborators. In developing a data "hub," we are not necessarily interested in virtualizing every system-to-system connection. Especially in the beginning, it's important to focus on the "vital few"—that essential data that people use frequently or for important tasks. By bringing people together to identify those key data sets, you are asking them to contribute to the organization's data marketplace.

Can you see why issue management, data modeling, and data virtualization are good candidates for collaboration? In other words, can you see how each exploits the IKEA effect? With each of these processes, people put some labor into the outcome. Each dataset that gets put into the hub, each issue that gets resolved, each layer added to the model, no matter how small, fulfills a need for completion. With these two components met, those who contributed feel ownership and a heightened perception of value over these key pieces of your data marketplace. With everyone working together, we can get our data off those islands for good.

CHAPTER FIVE
Data Knows Best

Data is more than a set of rows and columns. Data is one of our greatest advisors. It tells us what has happened and why, it tells how we can act differently in the future to achieve our goals, and it preserves insights for us to pass down to future generations. In this chapter, I will discuss how to capture and leverage the wisdom of your data, both for the business and for the data program itself. By reading this chapter and completing the prompts, you will be able to:

- ✓ Select assets and attributes to start governing metadata
- ✓ Understand a framework for showing the value of your nascent program
- ✓ Track the metrics that tell you something meaningful
- ✓ Keep zombie projects at bay and focus on high value projects

"Designed to make experts out of everyone": The Purpose of Metadata

In the 1930s, a "processed" food was largely an unaltered whole food that had been canned, pasteurized, chilled, or dried during mass production. [37] So when the Food and Drug Administration (FDA) began requiring "standard recipe" labels on packaged foods in 1938, its main purpose was to assure the consumer that they were actually buying what they thought they were buying.[38] But even this minimalist effort irked some high-profile politicians and by the early 1970s, the FDA had decided it was no longer in the business of declaring food real or "imitation."

The voluntary labeling practices of the '70s were, unsurprisingly, far from standard. In subsequent decades, food companies littered supermarket shelves with words like "diet" and "healthy," unburdened by any requirement to back those claims with evidence. Finally, we entered the modern age of nutritional labeling when the FDA was back in the business of consumer education. The standardized Nutrition Facts label introduced in the 1990s allow us to peer—if opaquely—into the make-up of our packaged foods. With these labels we can, if we are so inclined, alter our intake. The standard nutrition label didn't solve America's health problems. But that wasn't really the point, was it?

The point of labeling, and of describing things in general, is that consumers can make informed decisions about how, and whether, to use a product.

What is Metadata?

The classic definition for metadata is that it is "data about data." Metadata could be a definition for a data field or a constraint on what type a piece of data can take (like a number or a string). When we defined our 3 Ss of Data Governance—stewards, standards, and systems of record (refer to Chapter 3)—we were talking about three of the most critical pieces of metadata. Documenting metadata is an important step toward getting people to trust your team, your processes, and the data itself.

Functionally speaking, metadata management is the discipline through which data becomes understood and useable. This has both a human component and a machine component. That is, we can describe our data in such a way that it becomes interpretable by humans, and we can describe it in a way that it becomes interpretable by machines. In the former, we would collect business, logical, or semantic metadata. The conceptual data modeling discussed in Chapter 4 is an example of this type of metadata. Other examples include business terms, usage rules, and steward assignments. To benefit machine interpretability, we'd focus on physical or technical metadata. You would find this type of metadata in a typical data dictionary, as it describes how the data is structured and stored.

Of course, as AI makes machines increasingly human-like, the distinction between business and technical metadata becomes less important. Indeed, both types of metadata are requisite to creating artificial intelligence and machine learning models. Physical or technical metadata eases the data cleaning and transformation process, while business metadata helps AI identify useful patterns. These are just two examples, and indeed metadata is used in several steps throughout the AI model development, interpretation, and deployment life cycle.

Data Knows Best

Managing Your Metadata

Metadata management is a straightforward discipline in theory. Capture, define, document. On paper, it's routine. In practice, organizing metadata is often mind-bending. What metadata is worth capturing? What assets should be grouped together? When does a business term definition need to be agreed to by the full council, and when is it okay for a single steward to sign off? Documenting all of this can be all the more complicated if you don't have some type of data cataloging software. Nonetheless, I encourage you to take on this activity at whatever level is feasible for you—even if you focus solely on a small set of critical data and document its important properties in a spreadsheet.

Dewey Decimal Data: a framework for managing metadata

People often laugh at me because I work in technology, yet my favorite analogy for metadata documentation is that it is akin to a card catalog at a library. If it makes them happy, I will modernize my example by analogizing to the electronic card catalog. Whether you walk into your local library knowing exactly what you're looking for, or whether you're a browser like I am, the electronic card catalog is an eager helper. Whether you type in the name of a book, an author, or a genre, the results list information that guide you to your next decision: to go look for that book, a different one, or try your luck among the shelves.

The information I'm talking about here is metadata. What "data about data" do we care about here? Book title, description, author, genre, location in the library, whether it's checked out, related titles. All of this helps you decide whether you want to (or can) check a book out at a library. With the card catalog, the books at the library have become observable. It's not that we couldn't see all the physical books lining tidy twelve-foot columns. But that's the point: we don't want to see all the books. We want to see the books that are interesting to us.

What good is being able to see all the data? Help the people in your company find the data they need to complete a specific task. Give your data a description. Give it a steward and a system of record. Give it a quality rating and give directions to the spot in your "library" where it's kept. Give your data metadata.

If your data was on the library shelf, what would you put on its card? Using the business term "Gender," my card would look something like this:

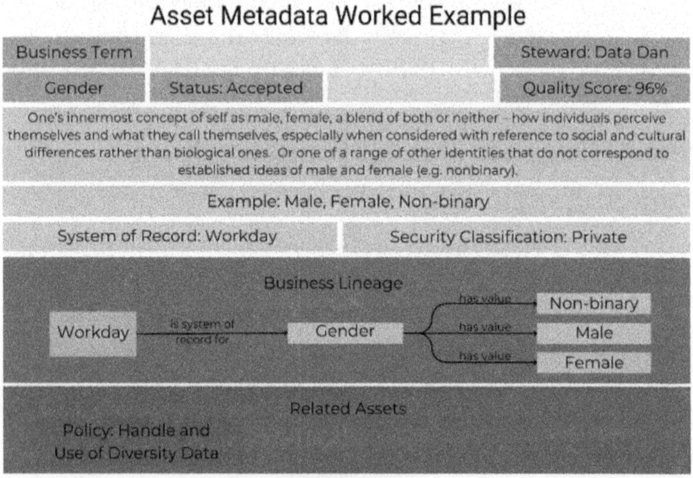

Asset Metadata Worked Example

Business Term		Steward: Data Dan
Gender	Status: Accepted	Quality Score: 96%

One's innermost concept of self as male, female, a blend of both or neither – how individuals perceive themselves and what they call themselves, especially when considered with reference to social and cultural differences rather than biological ones. Or one of a range of other identities that do not correspond to established ideas of male and female (e.g. nonbinary).

Example: Male, Female, Non-binary

System of Record: Workday	Security Classification: Private

Business Lineage

Workday —is system of record for→ Gender —has value→ Non-binary / Male / Female

Related Assets

Policy: Handle and Use of Diversity Data

Figure 29

If you needed to analyze pay equity among genders at your company, would finding this asset card help you get started? Would it help you get unstuck? Could it help you explain how reliable this data, and therefore the findings of your analysis, are to your stakeholders? Just like in a physical library, this little card does a lot of work.

We should all feel well-acquainted with metadata "must haves" by now. Even if you don't capture everything that I put on my card, you at least need to capture the 3 Ss: stewards, standards, and systems of record.

Whether you're going minimal or capturing a more comprehensive set of metadata, do future-you a favor and craft a document of standards and best practices for your metadata (would this be meta-metadata?). As general rules for our business terms, I like to follow University of Texas Journalism Professor Dewitt Reddick's lead. Reddick suggests that good definitions contain at least two of the following features.

1. A reference to the larger class of things to which the defined object belongs

2. An explanation of how the thing defined differs from other members of the larger class

3. An illustration

When combined with tactical business term requirements (like those shown in "Insight: Business Term Standards") these principles result in a clear set of guidelines any one can use to propose business terms that meet a central data governance team's quality expectations.

Insight

Business Terms Standards

<u>Required Attributes</u>
- **Name:** All business term names should have a business-friendly title. (i.e. no camelCase).
- **Definition:** If a definition contains another business term or acronym then the relationship to that term should exist. A business term should also be a clear and concise description with business-friendly language and proper grammar.
- **Security Classification:** A security classification is required for each business term. Must choose from one of the values: Private, Restricted, Internal, Public.
- **Business Steward:** Every asset must have a designated person responsible for its quality and to answer questions that arise about its usage.
- **System of Record:** Each asset must have one system of record.

<u>Recommended Attributes</u>
- **Data Asset Mapping (technical):** It is recommended to have business terms and physical columns mapped to each other so analysts are assured they are using the correct term in reporting.
- **Descriptive Example:** Provide an example of an asset being used to improve understanding of how a standard applies.
- **Notes:** Document any other guidance that would improve understanding of how to use a data asset.

Optional Attributes
- **Effective Start / End Date:** If a data asset is no longer in use, or if it is otherwise important to know when an asset was in use, the asset's effective date should be recorded.
- **Inclusion Scenario:** If a standard applies only in certain circumstances, note which data is subject to the rule and when.
- **Geography:** If any terms, rules, or standards are geography-specific, note the relevant geography.
- **Synonyms:** List any other words a term might be known by.

Capturing metadata no more guarantees that people will use data the right way than Nutrition Labels guarantee people will make healthy food choices. Reporting in 1994, a CBS Nightly News anchor described the new nutrition labeling requirements as "designed to make experts out of everyone." Thirty years on, I think a more reasonable sentiment for this and other types of metadata labeling is that it is designed to put expertise within everyone's reach. Lying ahead is the hard work of getting folks to reach out and grasp it.

Measuring Success

When it comes to understanding whether your efforts have been successful, there are two elements you have to consider. Of course, you will need to identify the instruments you will use to analyze data about your program. Before you start measuring, though, you must define what success looks like for you.

If I'm being honest, the question of "measuring success" is one of my least favorites. Maybe it's because it feels like it distracts from doing "actual work." Maybe it's because no one can agree on the best way to do it. We're often asked to define measures of success for a project or program ("how will we know we've done a good job?")—which is undoubtedly an important question. But we usually fall short either of the measure, or of capturing the information needed to assess the measure.

What's more, the measures we choose never really seem to reflect the actual core of what we are trying to do. This is especially true of "community" based measures like engagement, support, or sentiment. Perhaps much of the tension I feel around this question is that I was always taught that "you can't improve what you don't measure." But, so often, success is a feeling. It's not a number or a checked box. It's an impermanent feeling that you've done something right—and that others agree.

Defining "success"

Notwithstanding my discomfort with the topic, I have found ways to judge the extent to which I've aligned my work with the business's goals and whether my contributions have added value. In particular, I think about success (or "value") as a three-tiered framework that I call the "Foundations—Values—Measures" hierarchy.

As you move through the hierarchy, you can define your value proposition at increasing levels of specificity. Your Foundations are the broadest means by which anyone might provide value to the organization. No need to recreate the wheel here: plenty of frameworks exist, as I will soon discuss. Your Values, on the other hand, are personally tailored to your program. Within each Foundation you employ, what Values will you strive for? Ideally, these will be uniquely identifiable as a Value for your program. That is, if we folded a bunch of Values statements and put them into a bowl, would someone be able to pick yours out of the bowl and correctly guess it was yours?

Values will be less specific than Measures, which are the

metrics many of us are most familiar with. These aim to track the health of a particular piece of a program or activity.

Foundations

As mentioned, you don't need to get too creative in defining the Foundations you will use to gage success, as many frameworks already exist. In fact, the most simplistic approach might just aim to improve each side of the balance sheet (i.e., your data program will lower costs and raise revenue).

While both costs and revenue are fundamental to a profitable business, not every department has a direct relationship with revenue. Further, designing Foundations that center solely around finances all but guarantee that you will frequently fall short.

Starting a new department or initiative takes money. You may operate in the hole for years. Does that mean the data program was a bad financial investment? Not at all. Done well, it lowers operating costs for an organization considerably, and can both directly and indirectly generate revenue. But much of what happens in your organization financially is not in your control. Markets shift, buying patterns change, and other departments will continue to operate independently. Additionally, until you have hard data to back up your claims, many of your early estimates of financial gain from data-related activities will be hypothetical projections. That is, the organization may understand the financial benefit of the data program from the outset, but it won't necessarily feel it until those projections have had time to mature.

For these reasons, I've latched on to a framework that posits four ways of delivering value to your customers: (1) make them money; (2) save them money; (3) help them rest easy at night; and (4) make them look good.[39] Notice this framework maintains the key monetary drivers of success, but it also provides two other pathways to value.

How might a data program help your internal customers rest easier at night? Can you make them less worried about a data breach? About complying with a new data protection regulation? Can you lessen the feeling of overwhelm they feel when they need to find data to build a report? How might your data program make your customers look good? Can insights from data be drawn so quickly that a partner can instantly answer a client's question while they are on the phone?

Superior data programs will find a way to optimize all four levers. But it's likely that some will take longer to mature than others. Can you start with pulling two levers—one monetary and one non-monetary? How might you do that?

Values

You are likely already familiar with the concept of organizational Values. Indeed, I am willing to bet your organization has already defined Values or "service promises" for itself. In such a case as this, you will want to ensure your team Values align with those of your organization. But aside from that, your Values should be uniquely identifiable as your team's, in contrast with the more general Foundations described above. Your Values should also help guide you when you reach a fork in the road. If you need to choose between multiple options, ask yourself which path most closely aligns with your Values.

Again, plenty of research already exists to help you craft great Values statements. How and why to draft these statements in the general sense are beyond the scope of this book. Instead, I will analyze examples of Values statements that work. For those who are unfamiliar with the concept of Values statements, I've included links to research in this book's Selected Resources section (see Chapter 7).

Before we jump into analyzing data team-specific Values, let's look at an example of what I think are some of the best directional Values statements out there: Google's "Ten things we know to be true." Without opining on whether Google has lived up to its Values, its statements (excerpted below) give a clear vision of how the Values show up in the products Google provides, what a day in the office might look like for a Google employee, and how decision makers might lean on these Values when faced with tough choices.

INSIGHT

"Ten things we know to be true"
(passages excerpted from the original)

1. **Focus on the user and all else will follow.**
   Since the beginning, we've focused on providing the best user experience possible. . .Our homepage interface is clear and simple, and pages load instantly. Placement in search results is never sold to anyone, and advertising is not only clearly marked as such, it offers relevant content and is not distracting. [W]e believe [our apps] should work so well you don't have to consider how they might have been designed differently.

2. **It's best to do one thing really, really well.**
   We do search. Our dedication to improving search helps us apply what we've learned to new products, like Gmail and Google Maps. Our hope is to bring the power of search to previously unexplored areas, and to help people access and use even more of the ever-expanding information in their lives.

3. **Fast is better than slow.**
   We know your time is valuable, so when you're seeking an answer on the web you want it right away–and we aim to please. We may be the only people in the world who can say our goal is to have people leave our website as quickly as possible.

4. **Democracy on the web works.**
   Google search works because it relies on the millions of individuals posting links on websites to help determine which other sites offer content of value. We assess the importance of every web page using more than 200 signals and a variety of techniques, including our patented PageRank™ algorithm, which analyzes which sites have been "voted" to be the best sources of information by other pages across the web.

5. **You don't need to be at your desk to need an answer.**
   The world is increasingly mobile: people want access to information wherever they are, whenever they need it. We're pioneering new technologies and offering new solutions for mobile services that help people all over the globe to do any number of tasks on their phone.

6. **You can make money without doing evil.**
   To ensure that we're ultimately serving all our users (whether they are advertisers or not), we have a set of guiding principles for our advertising programs and practices:

- We don't allow ads to be displayed on our results pages unless they are relevant where they are shown.
- We don't accept pop–up advertising, which interferes with your ability to see the content you've requested.
- Advertising on Google is always clearly identified as a "Sponsored Link," so it does not compromise the integrity of our search results.

7. **There's always more information out there.**
   Once we'd indexed more...pages on the internet than any other search service, our engineers turned their attention to information that was not as readily accessible. [O]ur researchers continue looking into ways to bring all the world's information to people seeking answers.

8. **The need for information crosses all borders.**
   Our company was founded in California, but our mission is to facilitate access to information for the entire world, and in every language. To that end, we have offices in more than 60 countries, maintain more than 180 internet domains, and serve more than half of our results to people living outside the United States.

9. **You can be serious without a suit.**
   Our founders built Google around the idea that work should be challenging, and the challenge should be fun. We believe that great, creative things are more likely to happen with the right company

culture–and that doesn't just mean lava lamps and rubber balls. There is an emphasis on team achievements and pride in individual accomplishments that contribute to our overall success.

10. **Great just isn't good enough.**
    We see being great at something as a starting point, not an endpoint. We set ourselves goals we know we can't reach yet, because we know that by stretching to meet them we can get further than we expected. Through innovation and iteration, we aim to take things that work well and improve upon them in unexpected ways...Even if you don't know exactly what you're looking for, finding an answer on the web is our problem, not yours.

SOURCE: *Google*

What I like about Google's Values is that they might read like a feel-good after school special, but they actually reveal distinct choices Google makes to acquire customers, retain loyalty, and develop new products. Now, you don't need to state your Values quite as expansively, or explicitly, as Google has. Let's revisit the example mission statement from Chapter 3 to see how you might weave your Values into your data team's mission or strategy document. See if you can spot the Values in "Insight: Example Data Governance Mission Statement (part 1)" and how they would help make decisions about which projects to take on and how to approach change. Try it yourself first, and then we'll do it together.

Insight

Example Data Governance Mission Statement (part 1)

Our mission—To make our firm the model of a modern, data-intelligent enterprise for law firms and legal departments around the world by focusing on transparency, authenticity, clarity, and consistency in everything we do.

Okay, now let's pull out the Values together (see "Insight: Example Data Governance Mission Statement (part 2)".

Insight

Example Data Governance Mission Statement (part 2)

Our mission—Let's break this down line by line. Underneath each underlined snippet from the Mission Statement in part 1, read the insights explaining how I packed a comprehensive set of values into a single sentence.

<u>To make our firm the **model**</u>
- we want to be so good that others can use our methods as a template for their own data programs. This doesn't require us to be the first to do something, nor does it require that others must have the exact conditions we had to replicate our success.

Rather, we want to be the most effective at building imitate-able structures and processes so that the whole industry moves forward.

of a **modern,**
- because the legal industry tends to be about 10 years behind a lot of technical advancements, I wanted to call out that our team wasn't just interested in upgrading what we had. We wanted to be able to keep pace with the capabilities of other contemporary organizations outside of legal.

data-intelligent enterprise
- many organizations say they want to be "data driven," sending the message that they will make decisions not based on gut feel, but by following where the data leads. I think this is almost the right way to think about things. The term "data driven" implies passivity from the decision makers: they are not deciding, but rather being driven to a decision. I argue that there is still a place for nuance and gut feel in decision making. Can we be truly data literate enough to be able to discern what the data is and is not telling us? What it can and cannot predict? And can we fill in the gaps by drawing on our own experience?

for **law firms and legal departments** around the world
- although our framework is generalizable to most organizations, myriad problems remain that are unique to the legal industry. This is a big reason many legal organizations fail to realize the benefits of disciplines like Lean/Six Sigma, Digital

Transformation, and Agile. Thus, my team set out with the goal of running data operations like an innovative company would, but in a way that also spoke specifically to the legal space.

by focusing on **transparency**,
- I believed that people would be more willing to come on board if we kept them apprised of what we were doing and why we were doing it.

authenticity,
- it's not always easy to ignore whatever is being hyped in the industry at the moment. But my team wanted to take intentional actions that were both relevant to our goals and didn't fight the wonderful firm culture.

clarity, and
- I truly wanted people to understand what my team was doing. We aimed to always be clear in our communications, but we also recognized that "clear" for one person might not be so clear for another. We therefore took on a default position that clarity comes from saying something, and then saying it again, and then saying it in two or three different ways.

consistency in everything we do.
- how could I ask people to trust us if they couldn't rely on our processes or decisions? I strove to ensure we were consistent in the application of our rules, standards, and processes, so that the anxiety of change wasn't coupled with the anxiety of

> uncertainty.

Values statements like the ones in these examples give you direction. By knowing what you want to be, you more readily know what you need to do.

Measures

Among Foundations, Values, and Measures, a discussion about Measures is where I'd venture many people feel the most comfortable. When you are defining Measures, start with a clearly defined question that you want to be able to answer. For example, "does my platform have more users this month than last?", "has my rate of billing errors decreased year over year?", or "am I spending less money on duplicate data storage this month?" Your Measures (which your company may call key performance indicators (KPIs) or objectives and key results (OKRs)) should be carefully selected so that you are tracking something that is 1) meaningful, 2) knowable, and 3) unambiguous.

Make it meaningful

Surely we all know, logically, that we should only spend time capturing metrics that are meaningful. Something is meaningful if it provides insight and direction into something you care about. But it's not always straightforward what's meaningful and what isn't.

For instance, I could measure the percentage of my firm that uses our data catalog daily. That might seem like it tells me something meaningful—after all, I care whether the catalog, and the metadata within it, is adopted. But do I really care how much of the entire firm uses the catalog every single day? Perhaps—but probably not on day one. While I want the entire firm to use the data catalog any time they have a question about data, not everyone in the firm works directly with data on a daily basis. In measuring my pool of daily users, I'm much more interested in whether those who create reports and visualizations, build system-to-system data integrations, or discuss firm data externally use the catalog daily (or near daily).

Make it knowable

Now, as much as I would love to capture data catalog usage for those critical roles, I can't. My data catalog doesn't show usage per person. It only shows a total count of unique log-ins. It would therefore be unhelpful for me to create this as a metric for myself because the result is unknowable.

Just like meaningfulness, know-ability isn't always clear cut. For instance, I could try to measure the uptake of my catalog among critical roles in another way. I could poll the people in those roles. But people could inaccurately respond to a poll—if they respond at all. This makes polls a less-than-ideal way of measuring participation (as we'll discuss in detail soon). Maybe I could track the reports they put out and see what proportion use the data correctly. But what would that tell me? It would tell me only that the data was used correctly. It tells me nothing about how the report generator arrived at the correct data. Maybe they used the catalog—but maybe they didn't. Sometimes things we want to know are hard to know and we will have to use indicators instead of direct evidence.

Just a word of caution: the farther away you are from that direct evidence, the more out on a limb you are. The more out on a limb you are, the less you really know for sure.

Make it unambiguous

Finally, what we measure must be unambiguous. Let's take my first example measure "does my platform have more users this month than last?" and apply it to my data catalog. Depending on their role, someone could interact with the data catalog in several ways. They can propose new business terms; they can approve the addition of new data assets; and they can browse and search for data sets, business terms, and policies. If a person is on the data governance council, and they've logged in only to search for a policy, but have not participated in the approval of new assets as is their duty, do I count that as a "use"? If someone just logs in, but does nothing, is that a "use"?

I can get around this ambiguity by tweaking this general question into a more specific one: "how many people have proposed a new business term this month versus last month?" Not only is the rephrased question unambiguous, it is knowable, and answering it tells me something meaningful about the usage of my catalog.

The goal of this Foundations-Values-Measures hierarchy is to have a success framework that is structured, yet flexible. Then, when things inevitably don't go according to your plan, you can still find your way to success. In such a situation, you will be able to reason that, perhaps a Measure didn't end up where you wanted it, but you still delivered on your Values. Or perhaps you haven't yet lived up to your Values fully, but you still found a way to provide a benefit through one of the Foundations. You might say, for example, "I only signed 10 new clients this month instead of the 20 I had targeted (Measure), but I interacted with every client as if I were advising a close friend or family member (Value). This led to a deeper client relationship and more repeat business for the company (Foundation)." Or "My goal was to define 20 new business terms for our people data domain, but I only got through 10 due to an urgent data quality issue that came up (Measure). The depth of this issue caused me to belatedly reply to many of my internal customers (Value). However, because I took the time to fix the urgent quality issue, I was able to help prevent a public embarrassment for the organization (Foundation)."

Assessing your progress: Measurement tools

Let's now briefly discuss the instruments you might use to assess your progress toward your defined goals. You will likely have heard of qualitative and quantitative measurement, but there is yet another dimension to data collection and measurement. That is, you can measure things actively or passively. The matrix in Figure 30 gives examples of each type of measurement.

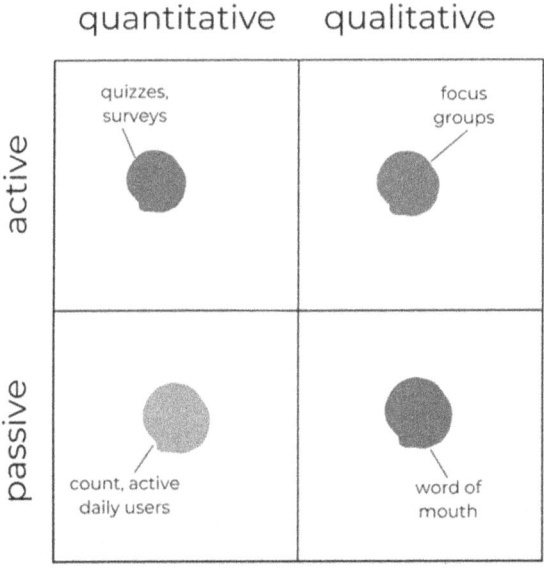

Figure 30

Certain portions of your program you can measure directly, and you could therefore use a method from just one of the quadrants in the matrix. An example of this might be if you wanted to know if your sales figures increased month over month.

This is quantitative information that you could collect passively from your point-of-sale system.

However, when you are trying to assess the overall health of a program, initiative, or product, using only one type of measurement rarely gives you a complete picture. For instance, active daily users on your product may be high, but depending on the circumstances, that might tell you little about the success of the product itself. Is its use mandated in your organization? Is it the only option available? In these cases, you may have great use of your product, but peoples' feelings about it might be quite negative. This leaves your product vulnerable to competition.

Passive data collection

Most people are probably comfortable with how "word-of-mouth" works. Word-of-mouth is the type of passive-qualitative data that we get through hearing (or seeing) what others say about us to their colleagues. The benefit of word-of-mouth data is that it is usually someone's unfiltered opinion, and therefore an accurate view of that person's perception. The downside to word-of-mouth data is that it is difficult to collect systematically, and thus we can't generalize the findings to a broader population without risking a fallacious or biased interpretation (see Chapter 4, "To be Fair: Data Ethics").

Passive-quantitative data collection, like the automatic logging of transactions in a point-of-sale system, rarely suffers from the same problems as passive-qualitative data (like word-of-mouth). The downside of relying on passive-quantitative data alone is that it usually isn't structured to answer questions other than the basic "who did what and how often?". To explore more nuanced questions about our program and platforms, we often must turn to active data collection methods.

Active data collection

In my professional experience outside of academia, I have found active collection of both quantitative and qualitative data sparse. This is understandable: we already know that our colleagues and customers are busy and we don't want to add to their burden. But for something as important as an enterprise data strategy, everyone is better served when they are part of a consistent feedback loop. To get a complete picture of your program's health, actively collect data that measures the "4Ps": participation, perception, proficiency, and preference.

Participation

In collecting data like counts of active daily users, we've already begun measuring for the first P: Participation. Data on how many people show up to a training, how many create an account, or how many click a link are helpful metrics. As alluded to above, however, participation metrics don't always indicate how people feel about your project. For this, we will need to leverage our second P: Perception.

Perception

How do your constituents feel about the processes the data team uses to achieve its aims? How do they feel about the data literacy content you send them? How do they perceive their own growth relative to data concepts since you started your program? To be sure, measuring perception is a tricky business. Taking examples from our matrix, perception most often gets measured either passively through word-of-mouth or actively through surveys. What people are saying about you to others is important, but it's a slippery metric. Surveys and polls are better ways to measure perception.

Though inexact, I like surveys and polls for a couple of reasons. First, you can get feedback on the precise things you want to know. With word-of-mouth data collection, you are at the mercy of whatever thoughts came into someone's head and out of their mouth. A survey's pointed questions ask people to think critically about an aspect of your program, rather than spew a general thought or feeling. This leads to feedback that you can more easily learn from.

The second reason I like surveys and polls is because they are repeatable. Indeed, my team repeats a data literacy survey every year to see if peoples' perceptions of their—and the firm's—literacy has increased. Repeatable data collection like this helps to not only track trends over time, but also reduces the noise—or bias—that may enter less rigorous methods. In some instances, measuring peoples' perceptions either of a program or of their own facility with data will be enough. In other cases, you need to know whether your population actually understands how to apply a concept. Examples of this include harassment or security compliance training. In cases such as these, we need to test for our third P: Proficiency.

Proficiency

Having gone through at least some years of schooling, we are all familiar with tests of skill. We are surely all familiar with this in our professional lives as well where, as mentioned, an organization must show its employees have successfully completed a training. With all of this required testing, you might find a weary audience if you try to impose additional required training and testing. But that doesn't mean you should forgo all knowledge checks. I have found it effective to add two or three interactive questions in our data literacy modules that allow readers to apply what they just read about.

You could track these responses if you wanted to, but I kept the results private to the user. It might seem like one less data point for my team, but as long as users responded to the questions, our rationale goes, they probably have a more accurate perception of their abilities. Our surveys of perception, then, could reasonably approximate actual skill.

Preference

Finally we arrive at our fourth, and most frequently underutilized, P: Preference. We talked earlier in this book about piloting software, programs, and ideas. During these pilot periods, you can connect with your eventual customers to gage their preferences for different aspects of your offering. If you are piloting a data catalog, convene a focus group. Ask them how they like the layout and whether they prefer to see diagrams or text. If you decide to try out a new business term approval process with your council, would they prefer to give feedback on proposed terms on their own or as a group?

When measuring preference, it might feel like you are learning things only about the specific item you're requesting feedback on. But our colleagues' preferences can tell us so much about how they think, how much attention they have to give, and what they ultimately feel is worth changing their behavior for.

The Quick and the Undead: Pitfalls to Avoid

Back in 2009, Harvard researchers Mark Van Buren and Todd Safferstone (hereafter "Van Buren," for convenience) studied over 5,000 new leaders to learn what separated the successful from the ineffective by asking the new leaders' managers to rate the new leaders' performance against a 10-point scale. When Van Buren analyzed the results, he found one thing overwhelmingly contributed to the positive or negative review a new leader was given: the quick win.

Van Buren named this phenomenon "The Quick Wins

Paradox,[40]" but reading his reasoning, it sounds to me like a classic case of "get rich or die trying." Managers unsurprisingly wanted their new leaders to show value quickly—and those that did were rated almost 20 percent more favorably than those who didn't. But those new leaders who were labeled "strugglers" didn't earn that title because they shunned a quick win. In fact, they chased the quick wins—they just died trying.

Van Buren attributes this failure to five behaviors associated with seeking a quick win: over-focus on details, negative reaction to criticism, intimidation, jumping to conclusions, and micromanaging.

- **Over-focusing:** Cited as the most common behavior tied to failure, over-focusing on details shows up in the leader who is so bent on getting a quick win that they study every detail of a problem rather than rely on the expertise of their team. This frequently coincides with behavior five, micromanaging.
- **Negative reaction to criticism:** A leader falling into the second most common trap, responding negatively to criticism, views questioning of her tactics as an aggressive act by a change-averse naysayer. This behavior often appears with the third, intimidation.
- **Intimidation:** In this context, the new leader is so confident in the righteousness of her own mandate that she effectively shuts down disagreeing viewpoints, ultimately losing her the support of her colleagues.
- **Jumping to conclusions:** Behavior number four, jumping to conclusions, happens when the leader decides the solution before fully understanding the problem.
- **Micromanaging:** This behavior involves a leader trying to control, in an unnecessarily intrusive way, the manner in which their direct reports carry out tasks.

We can learn some general lessons from Van Buren's findings, the main one being to make change a collaborative effort rather than a solo mission. But I like this study because a couple of behaviors are especially prevalent in the data field.

Getting into the weeds (aka "over-focusing")

The first prevalent pattern in data leaders is getting too into the details—getting "into the weeds." Especially where leaders come from a technical background, spending many years in the weeds—troubleshooting code, exploring a problem inside and out, writing requirements—it can be hard to zoom out. This is understandable, but it's a danger for data leaders because data is not a primarily technical asset. It's a business asset.

Jumping to conclusions

The second behavior I've found common is jumping to conclusions. In an effort to get a quick win under their belts, leaders will largely bypass the problem discovery phase and jump straight into solution implementation. I've seen this happen a couple of ways.

Over-relying on a panacea product

A leader (or group of leaders) buys a technology tool that promises to solve big problems. "You can store all of your data in our platform and perform analytics right in the interface!" the vendor claims. "And it's a really quick and easy installation. We can get it done in a few days!" That's a great candidate for a quick win, right?

Falling into the copy-paste pattern

The second pattern that frequently gets data leaders into "jumping to conclusions" territory is what I'll call the "copy-paste" pattern. Companies value leaders with experience not because the person can come into a new organization and perform the exact work they did at their last job. Good leaders are valued because they can apply their experiences to the unique circumstances of a new challenge. Sometimes, we may feel that replicating a prior successful project will deliver us a quick win. We've done this project before, after all, so we've already got all the kinks ironed out. Unfortunately, things are rarely that simple.

Choosing the wrong problem to solve

There's another pothole on the road to a quick win that even leaders not burdened by bad behavior face. That is, you can lose the quick win game just by choosing the wrong problem to solve. You have probably come across some version of a common priority-setting tool, the effort/impact matrix (Figure 31). Our true quick wins are, predictably, those that produce a lot of value with minimal effort. Those new leaders that scored 20 percent higher on their reviews in the Van Buren study found a way to get into this quadrant. Let's look more closely at the matrix.

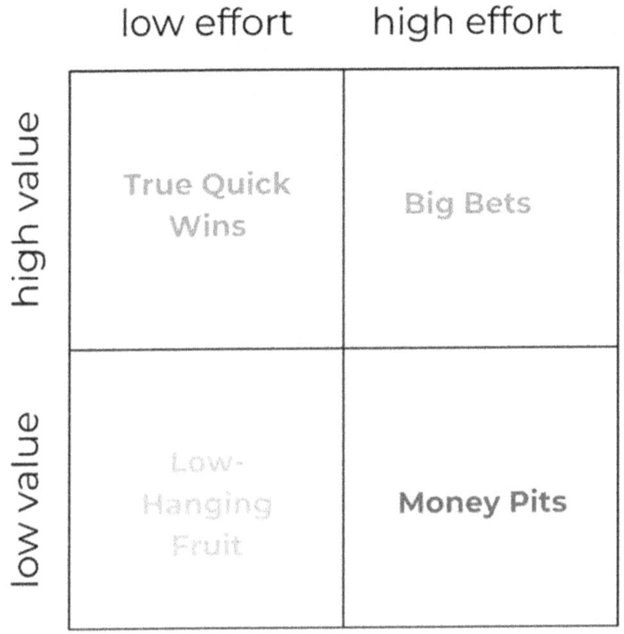

	low effort	high effort
high value	True Quick Wins	Big Bets
low value	Low-Hanging Fruit	Money Pits

Figure 31

From Big Bets to Money Pits

Work that is both high value and a lot of effort are called "Big Bets." This quadrant (Figure 31) is where you implement your overall, long-term vision and strategy. Big Bets are therefore the anchor of this matrix: whatever falls into this quadrant determines into which quadrants other projects fall. Why? Because in defining your strategy, you have determined where the value is.

If I've decided that my data governance strategy is to build a community of data citizens, I've recognized that collaboration is a valuable enabler of data governance. If I then hole myself away and create a suite of dashboards, even if it only takes me a few weeks, does that add to the value I identified in my strategy? Probably not. In this case, I'd probably slot dashboards in to the "Low-Hanging Fruits" quadrant. In a worst-case scenario, I'd buy an expensive data analytics platform and labor away for months trying to implement it, only to finish and have no takers. Now I'm in a Money Pit.

But what if, instead, I identified value in making insights quickly available to company leaders, and thus my strategy was to make data as accessible as I possibly could? Well, now my dashboards are looking a lot more like a True Quick Win.

The lesson of this matrix, then, is not that we get accidentally carried away with inherently invaluable projects. The caution is that we misidentify the value of a project to our business. But the value part—the "win" part—is still just one side of the equation. Don't forget that to get into the coveted top left corner of our matrix, the win can't just be a win. It has to be quick. Here's where our "jumping to conclusions" patterns come back to bite us.

Return of the problematic patterns

To demonstrate, let's return to our panacea-product pattern. There's a software tool, maybe one of the systems you already use, that has what sound like promising capabilities. It can take in all the data from your other source systems (your finance system, your CRM system, and so on), store it, and make it available for analysis and visualization within the platform. No more waiting on your colleagues for data.

Why doesn't this work? Number one, data is still going to be collected and—at least initially—stored in the source system (e.g., your finance system). So, you are either going to have to create a copy of the data, doubling your storage costs, or you are going to have to transfer and then delete the data from the source. This last option is, of course, a no-go because the finance team, for example, is going to need that finance data to execute other processes within the finance system, and they can't do that if you've deleted the data.

Number two, data can be stored in various formats: relational, columnar, graph, and document; JSON, XML, SQL . . . Even if you have technical chops, you could be in for a ton of work normalizing these various formats so they can be combined and analyzed by a broad audience. Number three, data may be owned by the organization, but individual departments and teams steward it. The finance team is the steward of finance data because they are the experts on how the data is, and can be, used. To extract value from any combination of this data, you will still have to work with the finance team to understand which data is valuable, which is private or restricted, and what conclusions can be drawn from any analysis.

Finally, so many major systems, from HR to finance to marketing systems, market themselves as panacea products. Given the prevalence of silos as discussed in the previous chapter, it often happens that two or more of those silos wants their system to be the panacea product for the organization. At best, this causes disagreement among departments. At worst, each department buys its own product, and you've got multiple expensive behemoth tools doing the same work.

Next let's remember our copy-paste pattern. Many of us in data roles are technical by background. That's why this copy-paste pattern is so enticing. We reuse code all the time. This makes us efficient—not wasteful. But no matter how similar they seem on paper, no two organizations are the same. Each has their own culture, data environment, and cast of characters. With that, you might find that a project worked perfectly at your last place but falls flat at your new one. You documented everything and if your new place would just trust your experience, you could get this project done fast. Why won't they just play ball? All of this goes back to data being, first and foremost, a business asset. We should lean on our experiences, but we must work to understand the new business context that we're in at the outset of a project, and we must adjust.

But let's say you've managed to implement a panacea product or copy-paste solution. Are you in the clear? Unfortunately, maybe not. The patterns described above are so fundamentally flawed that, once invited to attend to a promising quick win, they often breed zombie projects instead. Failed integrations, technical debt, and burned bridges leave half-alive systems whose effects interfere with progress years down the road.

Final thoughts on the quick win

Luckily, you already have the antidotes to zombie projects. Because you have thoroughly assessed the organization through the steps in the previous chapters of this book, you know where the value lies. Because you now know the common traps leading to slow losses, you can avoid them and instead show value by making quick win projects incremental steps toward your overall goal.

Should you take all this to mean that I don't think you should pursue quick wins? No—in fact, I think you have to. We all have to. That's Van Buren's lesson. Especially when our theories are relatively new, we are under pressure to show value—and fast. I also don't mean to suggest that your past experiences aren't valuable, or that you have to reinvent the wheel for the sake of novelty. And I certainly don't mean to imply that we must be single-minded. But unless what you're working on is an incremental step toward your overall goal, you're wasting your time. Before you know it, you've accomplished a lot and achieved nothing.

CHAPTER SIX
Data, She Wrote

Data literacy is not a spoke in the DAMA wheel (refer to Chapter 1, "Pieces of a Wheel: The Importance of Data Governance"), but it should be. If the people in your company know how to read, write, and communicate with data, they will be more amenable to your change efforts because they will understand the value of good data. While you can purchase third party data literacy programs, consider sleuthing out your company's data issues yourself, and then writing about what you find. This will make your content more relevant and familiar to your readers. Plus, writing about specific data topics, issues, and solutions helps you clarify your own thinking, sharpening your ability to spot and solve problems. By reading this chapter and completing the prompts, you are able to:

- ✓ Identify barriers to creating and sustaining change
- ✓ Capture your audience's attention with effective communications

✓ Prepare a data literacy curriculum that is tailored to your company's needs

Go Change

How many emails would you say you get every week? Of those not related to a task you're currently working on, how many would you say you actually read? Of those you read, how many would you say cause you to take some action or change your behavior? My guess is that we're fast approaching zero. And to be clear, this is not because we are lazy or stuck in our ways. If you've worked in a corporate environment the past 10 years, with rapid technological developments and new ways of working post-pandemic, I am willing to bet that you've experienced change and communication overload. As merciful as it might seem to spare your colleagues more emails, that truth is that you will have to frequently and consistently communicate your data initiatives, and their importance, to the organization.

To successfully lead organizational change, you must communicate, communicate again, and again, and again a different way. Of course, we know that it's not just about volume and variety: we must also communicate the right things, like why we are making a change and what we expect others' behavior to be.

I probably tell my son to "go change" three times a day. What I want from him is usually clear: change out of pajamas into school clothes; change out of school clothes into soccer clothes; change out of soccer clothes back into pajamas. We do this so often that I can usually get by with a simple "go change." Unfortunately, what we are expecting from our colleagues is not usually so clear. Yet many of us, me included, are guilty of pouring tons of work into a process or system and expecting it to self-explain its value to customers.

"Here, I've created this fool-proof set of guidelines for

using data that will ensure its quality. Now go—change. Change your behavior to match my expectations."

Personal barriers to implementing change

To frame our communications so that we avoid either confusion or irrelevance (or both), we first need to understand the personal (rather than technical, financial, or environmental) barriers that prevent others from meeting our expectations. You will have a good intuition for, if not hard evidence of, these barriers if you've followed along with the business-led data governance strategies introduced in Chapter 3. Barriers to change typically fall along four main patterns: a lack of coordination, skill, information, or enthusiasm:

- **Lack of coordination:** You will recognize a lack of coordination between teams when you see disagreeing business terms, duplicated data, and people from different departments trying separately to solve the same problems.
- **Lack of skill:** If folks draw inaccurate conclusions from numbers or present a misleading visualization, it's usually not because they have malicious intent. Where business intelligence and other types of data work are a "tack-on" to someone's day job, rather than their specific area of expertise, undesired results usually belie a lack of skill.
- **Lack of information:** So many data quality issues arise because a person entering data did not have all of the information they needed to input the data correctly in the first instance. This may happen because someone needs to create an entry before all the information is available, because they don't know what standards exist for the data, or because they don't know who to go to with questions.

- **Lack of enthusiasm:** Lack of enthusiasm can appear in a few ways. Your colleagues could be just plain disinterested in all this data stuff. They could be out-right hostile toward you: maybe you're encroaching on "their" territory; maybe the company has better things it could spend its money on. Or, maybe they would find your work interesting if they weren't already so fatigued by near-constant organizational change.

Overcoming barriers

Although the subject matter of your communication efforts will vary, you should find that at least one of these four barriers underwrites the current behavior. When you plan a communication, then, you should ask yourself which of these four root issues you need to address. For example, let's say you have a list of business terms in your data catalog that should eliminate confusion around which terms to use for reporting. Unfortunately, you've noticed that people are still asking the system owners which data they should use, or, worse yet, they are grabbing data without checking if it's the right field. You need to correct this behavior. What underlying issue does your communication need to address? My guess is that it would be either a lack of skill (because people don't know how to use the data catalog) or a lack of information (because people don't know the terms they need are in the catalog). Of course, it could be both.

Let's assume my guess is right. We need to communicate the data catalog in a way that corrects a lack of information and skill. To do this, I would probably draft an email that contained (1) a short blurb about what's in the data catalog (focusing on the data points I care most about), (2) a 60-second or less video showing how to search for a business term in the catalog, and (3) a link to join an upcoming data catalog training. Depending on the circumstances, I might also remind folks of any policy regarding the mandatory use of approved terms.

What if, instead, I drafted an email containing testimonials from others in the company who had tried and loved the data catalog? It's unlikely I would succeed with that draft. The testimonials would be a great way to increase enthusiasm for the tool. But I'm not up against a lack of enthusiasm in this scenario. If someone came up to me and said, "I just wanted to let you know that Sally really loves the whirlymajig," I would probably think "Good for Sally but I have no idea what that is." I would go about my day, unmoved by Sally's happy news.

To be sure, recognizing these patterns is just one part of understanding your audience and their needs at any given time. If I suspect low data quality might be due to a lack of skills, I next need to ask: what skills? What skills does the person managing this data need that they don't currently have? Do they need to learn how to identify data quality issues? Or do they need to learn how to properly ingest data into a database?

You can learn the answers to these questions through one of the data collection methods we talked about in Chapter 4 (see the section, "Assessing your progress: Measurement tools"). Or, if data collection is not an option, you can try to fall back on what you've learned about the organization through the process described in Chapter 3 (see the section, "Which data will you focus on?"). This line of questioning helps our communications avoid the string of email doom described in the first paragraph of this chapter. Through this process, you narrow down the universe of things you could communicate to your audience to those things that you need to communicate—and that will resonate—with your audience.

Sustaining Engagement

Now that you know what you're going to say, how can you say it in a way that will grab and hold the attention of your audience? Through my data literacy and change management work, I've found a few principles useful in sustaining engagement.

Create an identity

First, my team created our own brand identity for our products and communications. Creating a unique voice, standard color scheme, and even a mascot (Figure 32) quickly oriented readers and, as we provided more and more useful content, acted as a de facto trust mark. That is, our colleagues immediately know when a communication is from the data governance team, and they know they can trust that the information is relevant, necessary, trustworthy, and—dare we say—kind of fun. I encourage you to develop a brand identity for your team as well. Often your company's marketing team will be happy to create brand assets for you. They will also ensure your brand identity doesn't run too far afield of the company's branding guidelines.

Figure 32 © *Anna Busch*

Use visuals

The second principle I've found helpful is to be highly visual.

This can include increasing the joy of a communication with an eye-catching image. But we most often find this principle at work when we need to explain complex topics.

Humor me in a simple experiment that illustrates why. Let's say you are interested in the favorite colors of people on your team. You ask around and come up with this list:

Purple Purple Purple Purple Purple Green Green Green Green Green Green Green Green Blue Blue Blue Blue Blue Blue Red Red Red Red Red Red Red Red Red Orange Orange Orange Orange

Start a timer and answer this question: how many people like each color?

Stop the timer. How long did it take you to answer my question?

Go do or think of something else for a few minutes.

Are you back? Great. Which color did the fewest members of your team choose as their favorite? Do you remember?

Now, use Figure 33 to answer the same questions.

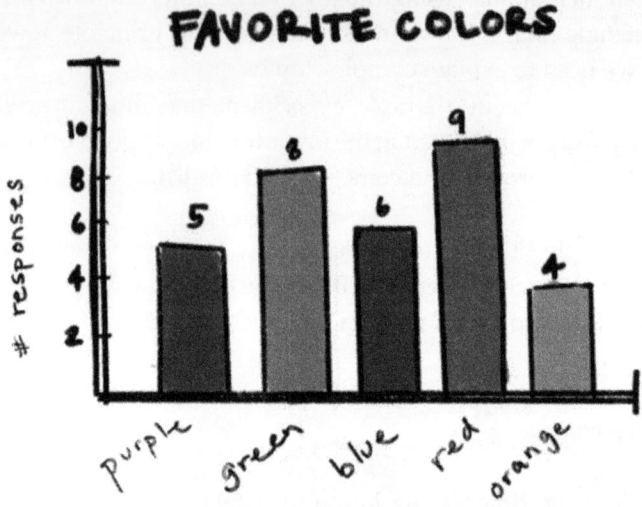

Figure 33 © *Anna Busch*

In which scenario did you have an easier time answering my questions? If you found it easier to interpret the chart than to read through the text, credit your biology. Our brains can interpret even unfamiliar images in as little as 13 milliseconds. To put that in perspective, it takes about 300 milliseconds to blink.[41] This simultaneous processing stands in contrast to textual processing, which our brains must do sequentially, word-by-word.[42]

Our brains process images 60,000 times faster than text — and remember them longer, too!

Figure 34 © *Anna Busch*

As our experiment demonstrated, we not only interpret images faster than text, we remember what the image taught us better than the text. Cognitive psychologists call this the "picture-superiority effect." The prevailing theory explaining this effect says we remember images better because we essentially store the image in two different ways in our brain. We store the image itself, and we store a word or phrase our brain automatically assigns to the image. With text, our brain only stores the words or phrases.

Use different communication formats

The third principle I've found helpful is offering a variety of formats. Email remains the primary method of professional communication, no matter how hard we try to change that paradigm. But that doesn't mean all emails are created equal, nor does it mean other platforms are useless. Even within an email, you can appeal to a variety of readers. Images are one way, as we've covered. But some of my team's most popular communications have been emails containing embedded videos—from a 10-minute interview series with members of the data team to 60-second quick tips on data catalog functionality. We also try as much as we can to put any learning as close in time and space as possible to the action it relates to. For example, if we want to teach our audience how to properly use visualizations to interpret data, an email or training module covering this topic is good. A pop-up or click-through guide once they open the visualization software is better.

Implement change in increments

Fourth, to combat fatigue and anxiety, change in increments. People feel the most psychologically safe when they are in familiar environments. When change is necessary, how might you communicate in a way that introduces some familiarity and, by extension, psychological safety? If you pair a new concept with one the audience is already familiar with, you can get your message out while providing a place for folks to retreat back to if they get overwhelmed. This is incremental change in the most obvious sense. Sometimes, however, you'll need people to accept a new value proposition quickly. But the opportunity to provide psychological comfort is not lost. In this scenario, how might you use language, graphics, or shared experiences to introduce new ideas in a non-threatening way? You could lean on the familiarity you've created with your brand, you could cut out the jargon and five-syllable words, or you could underscore your writing with subtle call backs to ever-comforting classic television shows.

Keep it short

Finally, be brief. Rarely should you say in two words what you could say in one.

Creating a Data Literacy Program

The pinnacle of my team's communication efforts came from our data literacy program. Though not part of our original plan, we chose to focus on firm-wide data literacy at the outset for a couple of reasons. First, if you can remember all the way back to Chapter 1, to the Gartner study showing why data management programs fail, you might recall that between 30 and 44 percent of respondents blamed a lack of skills and education. Second, in our initial discovery, which included a survey measuring peoples' perceptions of their, and the firm's, facility with data concepts, we found that folks weren't as comfortable with key concepts as we wanted. We needed to provide some sort of education. Unfortunately, getting a hold of a helpful data literacy curriculum felt like gripping wet soap.

Attaining a basic level of data literacy

The basic definition of data literacy is "the ability to understand and communicate with data." But this definition, though technically accurate, doesn't help us align our data literacy curriculum to business value. Just like computer literacy was vital to us and our companies 20 years ago, data literacy is vital to ensuring we are prepared to make the most of the next several decades of work. We hardly think about computer literacy anymore, yet we all need to know how to use email, word processors, and the internet.

In addition to the basics, we may acquire specialized knowledge in certain software or programming. For example, as a lawyer, I am proficient in using a product called Westlaw, which is a computerized legal research platform. If you're outside of legal, you may have never heard of Westlaw. But that doesn't make you computer illiterate. To take a less technical example, if I left Chicago and moved to Paris, am I literate because I know English? Or am I illiterate because I can't read, write, or understand any French? You might think "well, both . . . Or neither." I would agree with you. Why? Because literacy is relative.

Likewise, to attain a basic level of data literacy, we should all be comfortable with certain concepts. But we will certainly specialize. Data literacy is therefore a spectrum that is anchored by the needs of your business or industry. The question you need to ask yourself, then, is what is your basic French? What is your word processor? What aspects of data are so prevalent in, or important to, your organization that everyone must have an understanding?

Most organizations want their data to be high quality, handled properly, and available for use in business processes. What knowledge and skills would the people in your company need to have for the organization to realize these goals? If we take the data quality desire, what would people need to know to improve or maintain data quality? They'd need to know what the main measures of data quality are; they'd need to know how to identify quality issues; and they'd either need to know how to fix a data quality issue or to whom they should raise the issue. Taking the requirement that data is not misused, people in the organization need to understand guidelines for data privacy, security, and ethics.

"Where are my strikers?" Know your audience

In my experience, some data literacy content strays too far from what is useful for a general corporate audience, many of whom aren't even sure of their role with respect to data.

When my nephew was three years old, my sister took him to his first soccer camp. A casual, "try-it-on-and-see-if-you-like-it" kind of program, it was mostly run by volunteers. The soccer coach was fairly young himself, probably late high school or early college age. His precise footwork showed he knew a lot about soccer. The look on his face as he surveyed his new students showed he wasn't expecting kids quite this young. But, determined to run his game plan, he collected a breath, rubbed his hands together, looked at each of the kids, and asked "Okay—where are my strikers?"

I have to credit this guy for his optimism. But, if he could, I think he would probably tell you to plan what you are going to teach after you understand what your audience is ready to learn.

When we don't take the time to understand our audience, we can end up falling back on material that is interesting in the abstract, but inapplicable to our colleagues' work. I have, for example, seen corporate data literacy content that focuses on "the three types of analytics": descriptive (what happened), diagnostic (why it happened), and predictive (what will happen). But—and

I say this in the most literal, non-snarky sense—who cares about that? People who perform these types of analytics might care. People who request various types of reporting might care. People who receive reports and need to understand what they can glean from what's in front of them might care. But do they each care at a depth that they would benefit from spending 10-30 minutes with the material? The answer is no. First, if they fall into the data analyst role, they should already know the differences between these three types. Second, if they fall into any other type of role, they can quickly understand the distinction between descriptive, diagnostic, and predictive analytics at the point of contact.

Aside from the fact that this particular concept is quick to understand, it's also largely irrelevant to most peoples' day-to-day work with data. When we are talking about people in the organization beyond the data team, would knowing the differences between these three types of analytics help them meet their own goals? Would people throughout the company knowing the difference between these types of analytics even meet the organization's data goals? That is, would it help raise the quality of critical data? Would it prevent the misuse of data? Would it promote the availability of data as a company asset?

What to include in your data literacy program

What, then, should appear in a data literacy curriculum? As is the favored response: it depends. It depends on what the people in your organization need to know to enhance their work with data. In general, to be considered data literate, a person needs to be able to understand what inferences can be drawn from a set of data and how to draw them, how to spot data quality and ethics issues, how to ask probing questions and back up arguments with data, and how to use the data resources available to them. You can use these topics as starting points for your data literacy curriculum, and then tailor modules so they are responsive to the specific needs of your organization.

In the next section, I will walk you through the process I took to identify and address these needs when I was setting up my data literacy program.

Case Study: Implementing a Literacy Program

In 2022, my team distributed and analyzed a survey to assess our firm's baseline understanding of data concepts. Using these survey responses, we leaned in on areas with the greatest potential for growth. Specifically, most people already agreed that data is an important asset, but fewer people were able to spot data quality issues or describe measures of central tendency. Wanting to ensure the content provided value for all skill levels, we segmented our population into five groups of learners. We then designed learning paths for each cluster, with the goal of meeting a specific threshold of basic literacy.

Audience Segmentation and Analysis

In addition to our practicing attorneys, the firm employs around 1200 business professionals across 20 offices. They are responsible for the day-to-day management, operation, and support of the firm. Our business professionals include departments such as technology, marketing, HR, and finance. As many of our business professionals work in hybrid or remote environments, our email communications are a critical vehicle to building community across business units. From our initial survey, we combined the quantitative results with the qualitative feedback provided by participants (for example: their department, job title, and perceptions of firm data proficiency).

We performed a k-means clustering analysis [43] and found respondents fit into five distinct groups. We then used the combined quantitative and qualitative results to apply user personas to each of these groups (Figures 35-39).

Cluster A

"I am confident in and content with my current abilities."

Goals
"I am a heavy data user, and I want to continue to innovate with data for the benefit of my team."

Frustrations
"I wish there were more streamlined processes for managing data. Lack of standards make it harder for me to achieve my data goals."

Recommendations
Include this cluster in conversations around process standardization. Show them results and focus their education on the current services that exist (or will exist soon).

Figure 35

Cluster B

"I was told

Goals
"I interface with technology, but data handling is not a huge part of my role. I am focused on solutions and outcomes. If data requirements exist,

there would be no math." let me know well in advance so I can prepare."

Frustrations
"I am frustrated by the many demands on my time."

Recommendations
Get this cluster up to a baseline understanding of the basic concepts, introduce the data management team, and key them in early if we will need their help on a project.

Figure 36

Cluster C

"If I had more training, I'd be a data management advocate."

Goals
"I am very focused on my role and how I contribute to my department and organization. I want to understand how good data practices can help me in my role. I want to understand what the current processes are, who oversees them, and how I can leverage them."

Frustrations
"I am frustrated by the many different needs, requirements, restrictions, and efforts around our data. I want clarity and results."

Recommendations

> The primary focus for this cluster should be helping them understand data management. This should include introductions to the people and operating models.

Figure 37

Cluster D

"I use a lot of data but need help to understand the basics."

Goals
"I use data a lot in my job, and I want to be able to examine that data more critically. I want to have a better understanding of the resources available at the firm. I do not want to get overwhelmed by advanced data science topics I will never use."

Frustrations
"I am often frustrated by my own lack of knowledge. I know what questions I want to answer, but unsure how that translates into data requirements. It is frustrating to have to rely on more 'data-savvy' people to help me reach my goals."

Recommendations
Present bite-sized content of basic data concepts. Make data coaching sessions available, or create a buddy system where these people are partnered with a person from cluster E.

Figure 38

Cluster E

"I am ready for more advanced concepts."

Goals
"I want to innovate with data and add value to my department and organization with data. I want to develop my knowledge and skill set, and I want to showcase my abilities."

Frustrations
"I am frustrated by the lack of sufficient, high-quality data, and the lack of resourcing for scalable data products. I wish there were more firm resources available to learn advanced data skills."

Recommendations
Provide this group with high-quality, easy to access data. They will appreciate the transparency and may often be involved in our processes. We should make advanced concepts available to learn, and we should build a community of citizen data scientists/analysts. We should also provide them a platform to showcase their skills.

Figure 39

We relied on these five personas to tailor literacy content to meet the readers where they were, but also inform readers of topics relevant to firm goals. Survey non-respondents were randomly assigned to receive one of the two communications sent. This served as a de facto A/B test,[44] allowing us insight into which communication performed better. To drive and sustain engagement, we packaged learning into clear and concise communications rich with graphics, interactive eLearning, recurring themes and characters, and clear direction on learning goals.

Goals and Objectives

Our goals for the data literacy program were to equip business professionals with the resources needed to adopt data as a key organizational asset, apply skills to their work with data, use firm data to make informed business decisions, and ultimately drive competitive advantages for the firm. We broke these goals into four specific, measurable objectives:

- **Objective 1: Demystify the firm's new data team.** Inform readers of the data team's purpose and main activities and how to leverage data resources. We looked for a statistically significant increase in average responses to related questions on our annual survey. *Note for all tests of statistical significance*: Given our scale of 1-5, a statistically significant result equated to approximately a half of a point increase. We used a t-test and a p-value of 0.05. Significant results indicate the population did not get more data literate by chance, but rather were affected by an external factor (our data literacy campaign).
- **Objective 2: Achieve a threshold understanding of important basics.** Many of our business professionals prepare and interpret reports for clients and industry surveys. They must understand what the data is (or is not) saying. We looked for a statistically significant increase on questions related to bias, inference, and measures of central tendency.

- **Objective 3: Create and sustain an engaged community.** Data and AI are constantly evolving, and we cannot afford to lose our stakeholders' attention. We wanted to see at least 75 percent of our target audience open the communication and Click Through Rates, the proportion of those who click on the module out of all those who see it, around 3 (0.7% higher than industry standard for email marketing campaigns).[45]
- **Objective 4: Deliver content that is timely and relevant to readers' work.** Readers are asked to rate the module and provide comments. We strove for an average of 4 out of 5 stars and comments where the sentiment was mostly positive.

To measure progress toward these objectives, we replicated our initial survey after the campaign's first year and conducted a comparative analysis. This data was supplemented by comments and ratings readers provided for each communication, as well as engagement data from our communication platform.

Content Strategy

Our solution was driven by the research and audience analysis as described previously. Our tactic was to drive as much organic engagement as possible, first because the trainings were not compulsory, but second, because adult learners are more likely to internalize content if they are self-motivated. Thus, we drew in readers with eye-catching graphics and interactive modules with knowledge checks set around actual firm problems.

The subject of the modules varied depending on each stakeholder cluster, but always focused on a centrally important topic regarding the firm's use of data. For example, we learned that quality issues were top of mind, and that we needed consensus around how to apply our data for external surveys.

These issues were addressed by the topics chosen for our April and June modules (Table 3).

FEBRUARY			
Clusters	Description	Learning Outcomes	Objectives
A, D, E	Roadmap of Data Activities	Understand data team's work and upcoming projects	1, 3, 4
B, C	Interviews with data team members	Get to know the data team members as they explain their roles and key concepts	1, 3, 4
APRIL			
Clusters	Description	Learning Outcomes	Objectives
B, C, D	Statistical Storytelling: Mean, Median, Mode	Ask probing questions about a report, allowing you to take intelligent action	2, 3, 4
A, E	Data Quality Spotlight: Accuracy	Identify and describe accuracy issues; ask probing questions to remediate accuracy issues	2, 3, 4
JUNE			
Clusters	Description	Learning Outcomes	Objectives
B, C, D	Statistical	Differentiate	2, 3, 4

	Storytelling: Correlation, Causation, & Context	correlation from causation, avoiding common pitfalls when interpreting cause-and-effect relationships from your data	
A, E	Data Quality Spotlight: Consistency	Identify and describe consistency as a measure of data quality; determine when a consistency issue must be resolved to improve data	2, 3, 4

AUGUST			
Clusters	**Description**	**Learning Outcomes**	**Objectives**
B, C, D	Making Inferences: Sample Size, Significance	Identify if samples and significance are used correctly in presentations, dashboards, and research	2, 3, 4
A, E	Making Inferences: Bias	Understand common sources of bias in data collection,	2, 3, 4

		analytics, and machine learning	
		SEPTEMBER	
Clusters	Description	Learning Outcomes	Objectives
ALL	Deconstructing Visualizations	Identify if samples and significance are used correctly in presentations, dashboards, and research	1, 2, 3, 4
		OCTOBER	
Clusters	Description	Learning Outcomes	Objectives
ALL	Year-in-Review & Survey Opening	Remember what you've learned so far; reminder of resources; request to take yearly survey	1, 2, 3, 4

As needed: Wins related to standards & quality; Team wins and new resources; Opportunities to provide input; Early heads-up when help requested; Update when new data set available; Practical applications of "wins"; e.g., cost savings, new capability

Table 3

Delivery and Implementation

We delivered the campaign through email, following our

firm's IT Communications Strategy and Playbook. By delivering relevant content in trusted, consistent channels and voice, we relied in part on our credibility to drive attention to this learning campaign. But, our professionals often get dozens of emails daily. We thus took a layered approach to draw in more readers, like including key messages in the email to capture "skimmers," and then providing more detailed learning in the attached modules. We developed each module using Python coding, allowing us to employ more features than email alone. We stored the campaigns in the firm's data catalog, intranet, and learning management system for easy reference.

Stakeholder Engagement

To ensure we delivered effective, relevant content, we consulted with our data governance board (C-Suite) and council (managers and directors) on the most pressing issues facing the firm. We developed our strategy in coordination with our internal Change Management Manager, as well as internal communications team to ensure cohesive, rather than competitive, firmwide communications. Most people in the firm had never heard of data literacy, and thus did not understand its importance. We overcame this by using job-specific examples in our modules, as well as contextualizing data literacy in the broader digital era of life and work.

Results

MEASURES OF SUCCESS TOWARD STATED OBJECTIVES				
OBJECTIVE	**MEASURES**			
1 – Demystify the data team for readers	*Quantitative*			
	Avg. 2022 Score	Avg. 2023 Score	Result (using one-tailed t-test)	

	3.182	3.974	Statistically significant result at $p < 0.05$, $n=183$
2 – Achieve a baseline understanding of important results	*Quantitative*		
	Avg. 2022 Score	**Avg. 2023 Score**	**Result (using one-tailed t-test)**
	3.077	3.554	Statistically significant result at $p < 0.05$, $n=183$
3 - Create and sustain an engaged community	*Quantitative* • Average Communication Open Rate – **84% (9% over our target)** • Average Click Through Rate (CTR) – **4.4% (1.7% higher than industry average; 1.4% over our target)** *Qualitative Stakeholder Feedback* "THANK YOU for these modules! The topics are informing my view of data hygiene, the awesome responsibilities of data stewards/owners, and using data in a responsible way. Keep the information coming and thanks again for your efforts." — *Security Governance, Risk & Compliance Analyst* "Well done! It is very efficient to have it in bite-sized and easy to understand pieces." — *Chief Talent Officer*		
4 - Deliver content that is timely and relevant to readers' work	*Quantitative* • Average Read Rate (10 seconds or more spent in comm) – **60%** • Average Skim Rate (2-10 seconds spent in comm) – **19%**		

- Average Course Rating: **4.7 out of 5 stars**

<u>Qualitative Stakeholder Feedback</u>

"Very informative and will be helpful to know as I build my Excel skills. When having many columns of data in which you are performing VLOOKUP on, you want to critically think about which column(s) would contain unique identifiers as described in the article." —*Legal Support Specialist*

"The content was easy to follow and easy to learn. The examples made the 'sleuthing' relatable." —*Intellectual Property Service Team Coordinator*

Table 4

The survey results demonstrate a correlative relationship between our data literacy campaign and increased perceptions and understanding of surveyed concepts. The communication engagement scores show a continued interest in the messaging, and they outperformed other technology communications at the firm.

INSIGHT

Example Data Literacy Module

Data Literacy 📖

Making Inferences: Accounting for Bias

10 minute read. For questions contact Jordan or ____.com

Meet Data Dan, your new Data Literacy pal!

Keep your eyes peeled for tips and tricks from Data Dan as you continue on your adventure in data literacy.

Data bias is all around us.

What is data bias? We say data is biased when humans bake preconceived notions (whether consciously or not) into the collection, analysis, or reporting of data. Data bias typically occurs for two reasons: (1) a **logical fallacy** (e.g., availability bias) and/or (2) a dataset that is **not representative of the population** (e.g., sampling or non-response bias). This might be due to an error in how the data was collected or analyzed.

Why is data bias a problem? Data bias can lead to **inaccurate, unhelpful, or problematic results**! We use data to make lots of decisions, ¬from budgeting, to hiring, to measuring client engagement and satisfaction. Data-based insights are a critical component of our business! Being aware of common biases helps ensure we are measuring what we aim to measure, and that our inferences are sound.

Data, She Wrote

> **Did you know?**
>
> One concern about artificial intelligence is its ability to perpetuate bias. Check out this article:
> https://www.weforum.org/agenda/2021/07/ai-machine-learning-bias-discrimination/

Today we are going to look through our telescope at the universe of data bias. Follow Data Dan as we explore three spaces you may encounter bias: in data collection, in analytics, and in machine learning.

Station 1: Data Collection

Landing at our first station...let's look at the first area where we might see data bias: during collection. Here we are interested in how survey questions are phrased, who is included in the response group, and how responses are collected. Let's take a closer look.

Selection Bias occurs when the sample was collected in an inaccurate or biased way.

Data, She Wrote

This might happen if we sample a **non-representative group**! Let's say we want to know how many business professionals at the firm have pets. If we only survey business professionals who have joined our Perkins Pet Parents resource group, it is highly likely that we will overestimate the number of total business professionals who have pets. Look closely at **who** data is being collected from.

Sampling Bias is a common type of selection bias. Sampling bias occurs when certain people in the population are more likely to be selected than others. This can happen when respondents are not picked completely at random. A common example of this is found in surveys conducted by landline phones. Because most people with landlines are older, the results are more likely to be biased towards the perspective of older people.

Imagine you're surveying your colleagues on if they drink coffee. You stand outside the coffee machine to survey 30 people. Think about who might cross your path: coffee drinkers! Remember: you want your sample to reflect the *entire* group you are reporting on!

Another example of this you might find out in the wild is in the world of online reviews. In my observation, those most likely to leave an online review are those who have either (1) had a *terrible* experience; or (2) had a great experience *and* are the type to leave a review. The experience *you* are likely to have is somewhere in the middle. Do you also take online reviews with "a grain of salt?"

Phew! Now you know how to evaluate sampling methods. Now let's make sure we asked questions in a fair way.

Response Bias occurs when participants respond to a questionnaire in a way that does not reflect their actual needs or beliefs.

Why would they do this? Perhaps the right answer wasn't an option. For example, you hand me a survey asking if I like Diet Dr. Pepper, but I've never tried it. The options were "yes", "no" and "neutral". I'm not neutral - the right answer would be "I don't know!" - but I select "neutral" anyway. This might also occur when "prefer not to answer" is an option on a survey.

Data, She Wrote

If you receive a report from which you want to make decisions (i.e., infer meaning), take a tip from Data Dan and ask...

1. How was the data collected? If by a questionnaire or survey, were the questions phrased in a neutral way? Were respondents given the chance to respond accurately?

2. Who is represented in the data? If using a sample to generalize about a population (e.g., the entire firm), have you checked that the sample fairly and accurately represents the population you want to learn about?

> **Apply it!** 📇
>
> The office is abuzz about a new study that came out saying that 60% of law firm employees love reading. You look closer at the study and find the options for response were "I love to read" "I like to read" and "prefer not to answer".

What bias does this represent?

- ☑ A. Selection Bias

Not quite. Try again?

- ☑ B. Response Bias

Correct! The options are limited in a way where participants might select the answer that does not reflect their true beliefs.

- ☑ C. Sampling Bias

Not quite. Try again?

We've seen how bias might creep into our data collection. Next, let's look at how bias can affect our interpretation and use of data.

Station 2: Analytics

Up, up, and away to our next stop...analytics! Data bias can manifest itself in how we report out and analyze data.

Reporting Bias happens when certain data is withheld from an analysis.

Let's imagine you are handed a report looking at how our workforce has grown over the past five years. The report shows a count of all the new hires for each month. It looks like our population has exploded: 10 new hires in March, 25 in April, 15 in May... We know the data is accurate, but can you spot the bias?

If you answered "data is being withheld from this report", you're right! You're missing information on departures or movement around the firm – critical context to the actual "growth" shown in this report.

Another example of reporting bias to watch out for is called "data fishing." Data fishing happens when the researcher has a result they expect or want to see, so they look only for the data that confirms that result. To counteract this: if you are doing the analysis, make sure you have your research question and methods defined before you start gathering data. If you find yourself deviating from that plan because you are not getting the result you want, you may fall victim to data fishing. To counteract data fishing as a report-receiver, ask if any data was excluded from the results and, if so, why?

Data, She Wrote

If you receive a report you hope to use as evidence in your decision-making, take a tip from Data Dan and ask...

1. Is there any data being withheld? Why?
2. Does the data support the question being asked?
3. What do I expect to see in this data? Is that affecting my analysis?

We've talked about data bias in how information is collected and analyzed. Now what about bias in systems?

Station 3: Machine Learning

In a galaxy far, far, away...or right at your fingertips. What happens when our systems and machines are biased? How can we tell?

You may have heard the common saying in the data world: "garbage in, garbage out". For our AI or machine learning, this means that the machine learning is only as good as the data it is trained upon. There are a few sources of potential bias in systems. Today we're going to focus on only one...

System Drift occurs when the definition of a term changes over time.

(Psst – this doesn't just happen in machine learning, but in all of our business operations.) Let's say we are running a report on the types of pets we cover under our pet insurance plans.. Five years ago, our plans only covered cats and dogs. Today, we cover all kinds of animals¬: "snakes", "rabbits", "gerbils". The meaning has changed from "only cats and dogs" to "all domesticated animals living in your home".

Data, She Wrote

Not to sound biased...but this is a reason data governance is important! (You can find the meanings of common business terms and acronyms at the firm using our data catalog, Collibra.) If we maintain and organize our data, we reduce the possibility for system drift. This makes our data more accurate and reliable.

If you're getting information from a machine, take a tip from Data Dan and ask...

1. How are each of the data fields defined? Have those definitions changed over time?

2. How is the quality of the data ensured?

3. Can I see, in plain language, how the model was trained? Do I notice any biased logic in the way the model was trained?

4. After answering the questions above, can I trust this result?

3...2...1...blast off! Now that you're able to spot data bias, you can be more confident your data backed decisions.

✨ You are a data star! ✨

CHAPTER SEVEN
The Twilight Zone

Even with the best planning, and the best culture, and the best people, you will run into situations that have you asking, "what planet am I on?" Sorry, but temporarily inhabiting another planet isn't even the worst of it. The worst part is launching yourself into orbit with your trajectory neatly calculated, only to find yourself completely disoriented by the unexplainable forces of pitch-black space. If you don't understand me yet, just you wait. But, like Google has it's *10 Things We Know to be True*, I also have a few things I know to be true. Consider these principles, and the rest of this chapter that follows, my way of helping you regain a sense of direction in those moments where you're suddenly unsure.

1. Duplication is bad

You have the same data duplicated in multiple systems or sitting outside of the system of record in a spreadsheet on someone's desktop. I know you do. It won't happen overnight, but you need to make it part of your strategy to reduce the number of times a dataset is copied. First, storing data is expensive. If you are paying to store the same data twice, you are unnecessarily spending the company's money.

Second, duplication leads to quality issues. We've discussed the imperative of pulling data from a system of record, but let's bring it home here. If you have a copy of a data set being pulled into to system B from system of record A, unless it's streaming, there is a period between updates where data in system B does not match system A. During that period, if someone grabs the data from system B and runs a report, their report is wrong. To make things worse, often when data is copied from system A, it's changed before it reaches system B. Someone changes the column names, does some aggregation, changes a data type, and so on. Suddenly data set A and B, once the same, live in parallel universes. When you are faced with a scenario where someone needs data out of a source system, you will usually have your choice of ways to accomplish that technically. Whenever possible, choose the route that avoids duplicating the source data.

2. The quiet part must be said out loud

Don't get strangled by your assumptions. Don't let bad design go unchecked. It may feel awkward in the moment, but speak up. You will likely find that others agree with you, they just weren't comfortable being the first to say something.

3. You can't build what you can't describe

This seems like an obvious statement. But if you've spent any time implementing a new technology or process, you have likely experienced the headache of sub-par requirements. In the data realm, we frequently run into a pattern where a group will ask us to "fix" data that is low quality or unworkable, yet they can't describe what "good" looks like. For example, if your marketing team wants help cleaning up their sector coding, they need to be able to tell you what a sector is, which clients fall within that sector, and how to rank a client's sectors when they fall into multiple categories. If they can't do this, nothing the data team does will give the result they want.

That's not to say that the data team can't help other groups define their requirements. To be sure, the data team plays a valuable role in probing the data to validate the picture described by the business. But so often, we start building a solution without the clarity we need. This results in scope changes mid-project, or long delays as we have to stop and analyze.

4. A job unassigned is a job unaccomplished

In a conversation with my boss, Mark, he recalled a meeting from his time as a young Staff Sergeant in the US Army. (In that role, Mark was responsible for training soldiers in both mission and occupational skills, and for internalizing the advice he got from his Master Sergeant.) This particular meeting involved the Master Sergeant coaching Mark on how to assign duties in an unpredictable environment. Though most of the specifics from that meeting have faded from his memory, Mark remembers the takeaway: it's not always possible to prescribe each step in a process. People must have both clarity in, and ownership of, the outcome they must achieve. "A job unassigned," he recounts, "is a job unaccomplished."

Though the stakes may be lower, this principle is just as true when it comes to managing data. If you want your data quality to improve, you must assign someone the task of improving it. If you want the business units to agree on a common vocabulary, you must assign someone the task of coordinating and mediating the process.

For the Hitchhiker: Specific Tools for Specific Problems

Even with all of the theoretical and practical knowledge you now have, problems will crop up that will leave you scratching your head. Don't be surprised if, after putting in a ton of work getting your team off the ground, leaders in your company still struggle to understand exactly what it is that you do. This is normal. In fact, even you may not be completely sure how all of these disciplines fit together yet. Don't worry: In this section, I've got you covered.

Problem #1: Business leaders don't know how to describe what your team does

Even if they see the value in theory, heads of other departments may struggle to explain to their teams exactly what the data team does, how it all fits together, and how it ultimately benefits the organization. Below are a series of one-pagers titled "Talking Points for Leaders." I developed this series to help my colleagues explain data governance, data virtualization, the data catalog, and the value of each. Further, knowing that understanding takes time, these one-pagers also provide exact language leaders can use when discussing data team projects with their teams. Use the following one-pagers as examples of language you may want to include in your own communications. (To download a free copy of these templates, visit happydatacompany.com/resources)

INSIGHT

Talking Points for Leaders
Talking About Data Governance

Help your team understand data governance and what it means for them.

The Opportunity

Thinking about managing our data often conjures up images of data warehouses, servers, and complex technical processes. Data management certainly has a technical component. But we can only get value out of our data and related technologies if we properly govern our data. Right now, our data is stuck in silos, and we often format and store the same data in different ways depending on the system. This makes it difficult to coordinate across groups and leverage data the way we need to. Such decentralization also makes it difficult to secure our data properly. Data governance is critical to ensuring a coordinated data management effort leads to identifiable business outcomes.

How to Describe Data Governance

Data governance's core purpose is to create and enhance business value by improving quality, availability, usability, validity, and understandability of the company's data. This means that we will work to create a common business vocabulary, set quality standards, and prioritize data literacy education. Data governance is centrally focused on people and enabling the outcomes that matter most to the business. Data governance should not be confused with information governance, although there may be cases in which the two intersect. According to industry standards, information governance deals with the governance of unstructured data—i.e., records and documents. Data governance, on the other hand, deals with the management of structured data, or data that lives or can live within a database or information system. As a rule of thumb, I like to say that information is "data plus context." These definitions resolve about 90-95% of the situations, but there is some gray area between what is "IG" and what is "DG." For these situations, the two groups work together to ensure consistent results.

Quick Facts
- Data governance is the thread that runs through other data management services (e.g., data catalog, virtualization, and visualization).
- Data governance exercises authority through an operating model comprised of multidisciplinary firm leaders (a board and a council).
- Data governance will be the main source of communication from the data management department.
- Though situated within IT, data governance is a discipline that runs through the entire organization.
- Data governance is not focused on governing all of the company's data. We are focused on critical data that is highly regulated, is present in a large number of company systems, or has been identified as serving a

strategic business objective for the company.
- Any questions should be directed to DataGovernance@YOURCOMPANY.com

Insight

Talking Points for Leaders
Talking About the Data Catalog

Help your team understand the concept of a data catalog and what it means for them. Discuss the data catalog in conjunction with data virtualization and data governance so your team has a clear picture of how everything works together.

The Opportunity

If you have ever searched the firm for a data set, it may have gone something like this: you ask a person you know in the department you think would have the data you're looking for. This person in the department you ask has part of the data, but not everything you need. But they point you in the direction of someone else in a different department that might have the rest of what you need. This time, you're lucky and you get what you need from these two departments. Unfortunately for you, each department stored and labeled the data in different ways. So you spend some time matching the formats of each data set. You generate your reports and are ready to share your analysis. But, before you can do that, a person from a third department tells you that the data you used is private, and you shouldn't be using it at all. The data catalog and data virtualization platforms upend this process, giving users seamless access to the data that is available to them.

How to Describe the Data Catalog

Think of the data catalog as akin to an electronic card catalog at a library. At your local library, you sit down at a computer with the card catalog open, and you type into the search bar the name of a book, an author, or even a genre that interests you. You press enter, and the card catalog returns a list of relevant results. You click on one of those results, say, a book title, and the catalog takes you to a page with data about that book: the author, publication date, a summary, where in the library it is located, and links to related items.

The data catalog is the card catalog for our data library. You can search our data sets and pick a data set or point that is most relevant to your search. Upon selecting, you will get a page with information about the data you searched for: the steward for that data, publication date, definitions for the data points and any synonyms, links to related items, and instructions for how to find the data in the data virtualization software.

Quick Facts

- Anyone can use the data catalog, though we expect to have around 60 "power users."
- Data sets will be divided by "domain," not by business unit (e.g., we will have one "People" domain with a master data set for our people, rather than an "HR" data set).
- Each domain will have a data steward, or a person who verifies the accuracy of the data and answers questions

about its use.
- Initial and ongoing training will be provided.
- Any questions should be directed to the Service Desk.

Insight

Talking Points for Leaders
Talking About Data Virtualization

Help your team understand the concept of a data virtualization and what it means for them. Discuss data virtualization in conjunction with the data catalog and data governance so your team has a clear picture of how everything works together.

The Opportunity

Right now, we have hundreds of data sources and systems. To function properly, each of these systems needs to use data from a number of other systems. This leads to a data architecture that looks like a bowl of spaghetti. The varied content and format of these sources leads to technically complex system integrations, data quality and integrity issues, and a frustrating experience for those who use the data. We are unraveling this bowl of spaghetti using [NAME OF SOFTWARE YOU ARE USING], a data virtualization platform. [SOFTWARE] creates a hub and spoke data architecture, where [SOFTWARE] is the hub, and the various data sources are the spokes. Because each system of record only needs to talk to [SOFTWARE] instead of the hundreds of other sources that rely on it, users can access the complete data they need (with access permissions built in), while we reduce the operational load placed on our other systems (and the folks who administer them).

How to Describe Data Virtualization

At a high level, if the data catalog is our "card catalog," then [DATA VIRTUALIZATION SOFTWARE] is our library. The data catalog helps you understand and locate the data you need, and [SOFTWARE] is where you go to get that data. In [SOFTWARE], we combine varied data sets into a single source. We certify the data sets and ensure appropriate access permissions before we make the data available to view or download from [SOFTWARE].

Data is compiled into [SOFTWARE] through "connectors" with the various data sources. We currently have a few connectors in place, and data from these sources are now available in [SOFTWARE]. We are continuously adding connectors to new sources. For a current list of available data, contact the Service Desk.

Quick Facts
- [SOFTWARE] is live and certain data is ready to use now.
- Our team is developing a user-friendly interface to [SOFTWARE], as right now you have to be quite technical to use it.
- The data catalog will provide instructions on how to get data from [SOFTWARE].
- Training will mostly focus on the data catalog, as that is the gateway to the data. We will provide some education around data virtualization, but it will largely mirror what is provided above.
- Any questions should be directed to the Service Desk.

INSIGHT

Talking Points for Leaders
Describing Value & Encouraging Participation

Reiterate the value of a centralized, shared data resource over redundant systems with siloed data. Describe the value of data governance in terms that are relevant to your team's primary goals and encourage them to participate in our initiatives.

Describing Value

Underscore that the firm will continue to have systems of record (e.g., Elite or Workday), but that these sources will feed a centralized repository (the data virtualization software). Emphasize the importance of centralizing by discussing the security advantages (e.g., accurately securing one system is less risky than accurately securing dozens), the efficiency gains (e.g., people will spend less time looking for and cleaning data), and the monetary benefits (e.g., maintaining many systems that do the same or similar things costs the firm hundreds of thousands of dollars—at least—per year).

The data governance team will regularly report out measures of value that it tracks as part of its program administration. You can make the benefits more tangible by describing the things that your team can learn or do better with access to better data. Below are some examples you might use:

1. Data allows us to evaluate whether our learning and

development initiatives lead to an increase in worker productivity and engagement scores.
2. Data helps us learn whether there is inequity in our compensation structure.
3. With data, we can understand whether the revenue a client brings in is worth the amount of work they conflict us out of.
4. Using data, we can increase client stickiness by providing data as a service.
5. Data allows us to assess growth potential for clients, practices, and geographies.
6. Data helps us ensure we are charging optimal rates commensurate with our value.

Encouraging Participation

The success of the data governance program depends on the participation of the entire enterprise. We know you and your teams are asked to do and focus on so much, so we keep our communications as relevant as possible. So, when we do send a broad communication, know that it is because we truly need your attention. As a leader, we hope that you will reiterate the importance of your team's contribution to proper management of firm data. And, when data governance requests participation in an initiative, please remind your team members to participate. We can craft sustainable policies that consider their expertise and ways of working, but only if they make their voices heard.

Problem #2: You don't have a data catalog

Not having data catalog software is not an excuse for not capturing critical metadata. OK, so you don't have the budget for a big name data cataloging software like Collibra or Informatica. What do you have? Do you have an enhanced spreadsheet program like SmartSheets? Do you have Microsoft products? Often an Office365 license will come with tracking programs like Lists—and it always comes with Excel. This is not to say that you will be able to capture everything you would be able to with specific cataloging software. But we're not here to be perfect—we're here to get started. Before I implemented our data catalog software, I tracked our critical data assets in Microsoft Lists. Take a look (Figure 40).

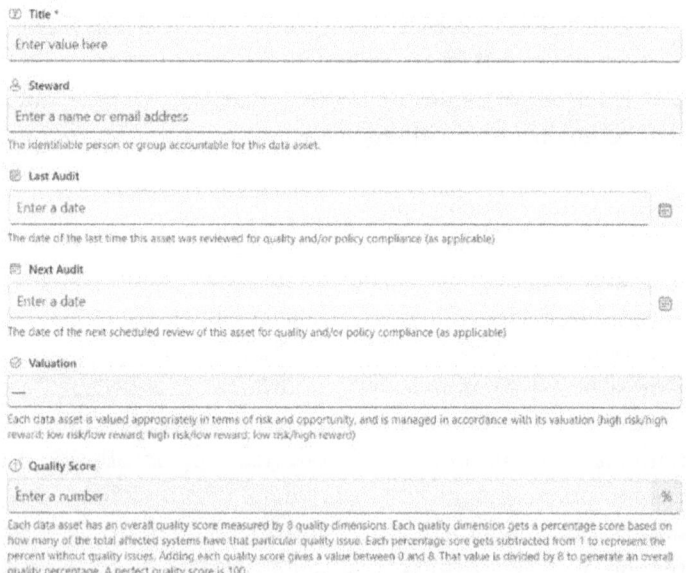

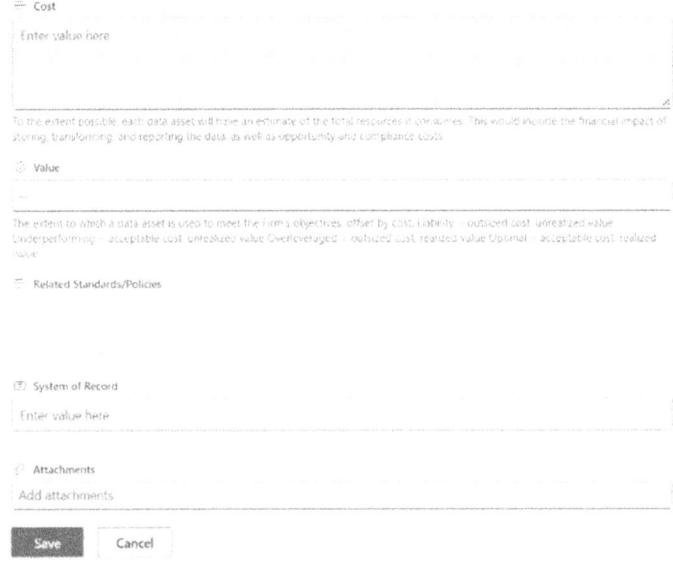

Figure 40

Problem #3: You can't envision how all the processes work together yet

Learning how the data governance process, the cataloging process, and the virtualization process all work together so that everything is done correctly but no one becomes a bottleneck is challenging. My team is still working to optimize this process, but we have found that using the below checklist helps us ensure we don't overlook any step.

Insight

New Data Asset Creation Checklist
Sample

Phase 1: Data Identification

☐ We have completed an initial valuation of the data set.
☐ We have identified and reviewed any relevant data governance council resolutions.
☐ We have identified the steward(s) responsible for this data asset.
☐ We have agreed-upon systems of record for all data comprising this asset.
☐ We have communicated any resources we required from the data steward to that steward during project onboarding.

Phase 2: Evaluation & Planning

☐ We have performed a technical continuity assessment, and we know what is needed to ensure continuity of service.
☐ We have performed a data quality assessment.
☐ We have performed a data security and privacy assessment.
☐ We have reviewed all existing standards and policies related to this data set and its uses.
☐ We have identified all relevant metadata for this dataset and have included this metadata in our requirements gathering with our steward(s).
☐ If we find significant quality, security, privacy, or other issues, we have put these issues on the list for remediation.
☐ We have drafted dataflow diagrams showing the movement of the data from the system of record.

☐ We have drafted a continuity plan to ensure technical work does not interfere with continuity of service.
☐ We have drafted a plan for connecting each system of record for this asset to the data virtualization platform.
☐ We have drafted a quality assurance (QA) plan to test our implementation before moving to production.
☐ We have created a plan to apply relevant security and privacy rules to our implementation.

Phase 3: Staging
☐ We have staged the data catalog with the agreed-upon metadata.
☐ We have staged the physical views in the development environment.
☐ We have gathered QA results (including customer feedback).
☐ We have staged the data virtualization scheduler.

Phase 4: Deployment & Abstraction
☐ We have communicated the readiness of the data assets for use to stakeholders.
☐ We have published all relevant data catalog updates.
☐ We have published logical views in the data virtualization platform.
☐ We have shut off redundant connections to this data from other systems.
☐ We have created a plan for ongoing monitoring and maintenance.

(To download a free copy of this template, visit happydatacompany.com/resources)

Problem #4: You're being asked hard questions

We've certainly been there. You want to talk about all the cool work you're going to do for the company, but you keep getting brought down to Earth by the same questions. Many of these FAQs are valid, so let's talk about how you might answer them.

FAQ: We already have a/an [Information Governance, Information Security, Data Privacy, Data Analytics...] Department. Isn't that enough?

Unless they are performing all of the activities discussed in this book in a coordinated way, probably not. Remember, data is a business asset, and proper management of that asset requires a holistic approach. That's why you're unlikely to get the benefits you want from data privacy or analytics team alone.

Also lurking in this question is an uncertainty about the difference between "data" and "information." I've said—and you may have heard elsewhere—that information is "data plus context." If this helps you, go with it. I like this definition better than some others that have distinguished between structured data (that which is stored in a database) and unstructured data (that which, I guess, is not stored in a database. Examples here might include text, video, and audio). Especially in the generative AI era, however, unstructured data is still data. And, I don't know about you, but I am not willing to accept that data is numbers only. Why tie our hands unnecessarily?

Well, now I seem to be saying that information and data are the same thing, so that information governance team your company has is good enough and you don't need data governance after all, right? Again, probably not. There's a distinction that I find more helpful than the structured versus unstructured dichotomy. An information governance team is more likely to focus on work product and the obligations that attach to it. I work in a document-heavy business where our work product consists largely of text files (motions, briefs, contracts) created for clients. In the course of representation, we also maintain other documents relevant to a matter (evidence, discovery materials, records). A firm has contractual obligations to the client with respect to this work product (e.g., to keep documents confidential), as well as other legal and regulatory obligations (e.g., legal holds or other requirements for retaining documents). These are the types of things an information governance team should focus on. That leaves a world of other activities (like those described in this book—and much more) for a dedicated data governance team.

FAQ: Is data management just another corporate fad?

It could be if you aren't careful. If you've spent any time in the corporate world, you've experienced the buzzwords and you've lived through the myriad new business processes that promise breakthrough progress. Surely some of you readers still shudder at the mention of words like "Lean," "Agile," or "Innovation." What makes me think "data-driven" won't meet the same fate in five years?

Who needs five years? I roll my eyes today when I hear "data driven" as a corporate strategy. That's what I mean when I say this work could become a fad if we aren't careful.

Lean process improvement, Agile project management, and Innovation work aren't fads because they are inherently unvaluable. They became fads because we either fall into the copy-paste pattern from Chapter 5, failing to properly tailor the principles to our company's culture and needs, or we implement them in name only.

Having sprints every two weeks doesn't make you Agile just like having an innovation department doesn't make you innovative. Companies that have successfully become lean or agile or innovative are so because they understood—and funded—the real cultural change that was necessary to derive benefits from these disciplines. If you focus hard on providing the

The Twilight Zone

services that your business needs, then it's not a fad, no matter how many times "data driven" is said at a conference.

FAQ: When will [the group I really care about] see results?

When I am asked this question, the group being cared about is usually partners of the firm. This makes sense, as the partners are the owners of the firm. And, granted, a lot of this data "stuff" can seem far removed from the practice of law. Like any other leader of a company, a partner might not immediately see how standardizing business terms, for example, helps them win more cases or make more money. You will have to draw that line for them. But think back to our Foundations-Values-Measures framework from Chapter 5 and recall that not everyone in your organization needs to have their hands on data to benefit from your work.

My partners, and the leaders of your company, benefit from data management and governance from day one. They benefit from increased peace of mind knowing we are more prepared to prevent and recover from a data breach. They benefit from more profits in their pockets because we spend less money on duplicate storage and perpetual data quality remediation. They benefit out in the market because your team can provide them targeted, data-backed recommendations for growth.

The benefits should become more tangible to your leaders as your data team matures, but that doesn't mean you have nothing to highlight early on. You just have to connect those dots. And if you can't connect the dots—if you can't think of any benefit to leadership or another key group in your company—then you probably need to go back to the drawing board and focus on projects that are better aligned with business value.

FAQ: Is participation mandatory?

The answer to that question depends on how important data management is to your company. I am assuming it is important to you, but not everyone in the company will feel as strongly. Whether it's because employees are already required to take so many trainings (harassment trainings, data security trainings, and so on), or whether your company doesn't have a general practice of mandating things beyond what's legally required, you will probably face hesitation if you try to mandate participation. That said, certain aspects of data management are worth the effort to mandate. Of course, any privacy or security efforts need to be strictly followed.

You should also mandate organization-wide compliance with the standards you create with your council (e.g., business terms or data quality standards). Failure to do so won't result in legal penalties as lagging privacy compliance might. But patchwork implementation will foreclose the benefits you covet.

For many companies, certain components like your data literacy content, lunch and learns, and beyond-the-basics trainings should be optional. Your hope, if not your goal, should be to get 100 percent of the company engaged in your optional trainings. But your job in this instance is to build an engaged community that wants to learn more.

Problem #5: You need to curtail poor data handling ethics with a policy

A good policy on ethical data handling instructs the organization on how to avoid using data to mislead or misrepresent, how to minimize bias, and how to identify high-quality and trustworthy data. The following is a template you may use as a starting point for drafting your own ethical data handling policy. This policy does not cover data privacy or security obligations.

Insight

Ethical Data Handling
Sample Policy

Data handling (how to procure, store, manage, use, and dispose of data) must align with ethical, as well as legal, principles in order to protect an organization's reputation, employees, and customers. Ethical handling often requires understanding of technical and statistical concepts. Please reach out to the Data Management team if you are not familiar with these concepts.

Introduction

[YOUR COMPANY] is committed to handling data, including personal data, in an ethical way. This includes considering the impact personal data handling has on individuals and guarding against misuse. The ethical principles in this policy aim to protect the firm and its people from inaccurate or unjust inferences as technology advances and data becomes more available than ever. We also take our legal and regulatory obligations seriously. You can read about our compliance practices in our privacy policies: [LINK TO YOUR PRIVACY POLICY].

Avoiding Misrepresentation
1. **Data fishing:** users of company data shall not selectively gather or report data in a way that distorts or obscures reality. Prohibited practices include, but are not limited to, cherry-picking data, omitting some data points, and strategically timing data capture at opportune times.

2. **Statistical smoothing:** users of company data shall not engage in misleading statistical smoothing, nor engage in "data mining snooping" or any other practice involving the performance of mass correlations on a dataset in search of statistically significant findings.

3. **Misleading visualizations:** users of company data shall not use charts and graphs to present data in a misleading manner. Prohibited practices include, but are not limited to, manipulating a chart's scale in a way that distorts or obscures reality (e.g., making trends look better or worse), omitting data points, ignoring accepted visual conventions, and comparing facts or groups without clarifying their relationship.

4. **Unclear definitions:** users of company data must clarify which definitions they are using for data in their analyses, especially where there might be multiple accepted definitions.

DO: Define the question you are trying to answer, and data sets and points you will need to answer that question before gathering data.

DO: Familiarize yourself with data visualization best practices.

DO: Fully explain your visualizations. A best practice is to include a separate document explaining that variables have the same scale, any relationships between compared groups, and any definitions or assumptions relied on.

> **DO:** Utilize the company's data visualization team!

Minimizing Bias
1. **Biased use of collected data:** users of company data shall draw conclusions that naturally and logically flow from the collected data. Users shall not manipulate data or its interpretation to make it support a pre-determined conclusion.

2. **"Hunch and search":** users of company data shall not use only the data that satisfies a hunch while failing to account for other possibilities the data may surface. Before drawing conclusions from a correlation, users should attempt to identify explainer variables that may account for the correlation (i.e., ensure you are not declaring causation when there is only correlation).

3. **Biased sampling:** users of company data shall, to the best of their ability, limit bias in data sampling by using statistical tools to select sample sets and by selecting adequate sample sizes.

4. **Cultural or contextual bias:** users of company data, especially where data is used in a decision-making capacity, shall make all due effort to understand where cultural bias may affect outcomes. Users shall further make all due effort to add context to data-based decisions such that data is presented and actioned in the most neutral way possible.

> **DO:** Define the question you aim to answer and your data collection plan before you start gathering data.

> **DO:** Account for other causes of a correlation beyond your variable of interest.

Ensuring Data Quality
1. **Quality dimensions:** The data team shall develop procedures to measure and improve accuracy, consistency, integrity, timeliness, and validity of critical data.

2. **Lineage:** The data team shall develop procedures to certify datasets and establish the lineage of those datasets.

3. **Metadata:** The data team shall develop reliable metadata for critical data, including consistent definitions of individual data elements, lineage, steward information, and protection level.

Types of Projects at Higher Risk for Ethical Issues
1. **Identification projects:** thoughtfully consider the data selection method and the demographic data needed.

2. **Behavior capture projects:** consider content, capture method, and any legal review that may be necessary.

3. **BI/Analytics/Data Science:** including profiling prospects and forecasting activities.

4. **Decision-making:** including granting or denial of permissions, status, or relationship changes (Note: personal information may not be used in automated decision-making without consultation from the data team and the company's privacy counsel).

The Twilight Zone

(To download a free copy of this template, visit happydatacompany.com/resources)

Problem #6: You need a policy addressing access and use of sensitive personal data

A policy covering sensitive personal data should include sections on the type of data collected, how that data can be used, shared, and stored, and how those in the company can request access to this data. The policy example below refers to sensitive demographic data, but the principles can apply to any type of personal information. This example is meant as a starting point only; you should consult with your company's privacy counsel to ensure compliance with obligations that apply to you.

INSIGHT

Sensitive Demographic Data Handling and Use
Sample Policy

Introduction
This policy governs the process for collecting, accessing, using, storing, retaining, and disclosing sensitive demographic data. Our goal is to supply our teams and customers with the data needed to perform their duties and objectives while protecting the Demographic Data (defined below) from unapproved uses.

The company is legally required to share certain protected personal characteristics for government reporting purposes. However, for the collection and disclosure of information that we are not legally required to collect and disclose, individual participation is entirely voluntary. The company will only use and disclose Demographic Data in accordance with this policy. There will be no adverse impact on employment if a member of the company declines to provide any voluntary Demographic Data.

Definitions

Demographic Data—Demographic identification information of an individual's race, ethnicity, age, nationality, disability, gender, veteran status, citizenship, and data related to sexual preference and/or sexual orientation.

Disaggregated, Non-Anonymized Demographic Data—Demographic Data that is provided on an individualized basis or contains personally identifiable information.

Personally Identifiable Information (PII)—Data that can be used to identify a specific person.

Requestor—The individual(s) asking for permission to download, use, and store Disaggregated, Non-Anonymized Demographic Data.

Approver—The individual(s) granting or denying permission to download, use, and store Disaggregated, Non-Anonymized Demographic Data.

Data Governance Team ("DGT")—The team, led by the Data Governance Manager, comprising data governance personnel and activities at the company.

Denodo—The company's data virtualization platform. Denodo centralizes numerous data sources and makes them easily accessible.

DMS—The company's document management system.

Collibra—the company's data catalog, owned and maintained by the DGT.

Information Collected

As part of our diversity and inclusion initiatives, the company may collect certain data points that an individual voluntarily provides through a demographic data questionnaire in our human resources system. The information requested includes an individual's:
- Age
- Race and ethnicity
- Disability
- National origin
- Gender
- Sexual orientation
- Immigration status
- Veteran status

Some demographic information is required for benefit providers and legally mandated reporting. Outside of those characteristics, an individual's choice to provide Demographic Data is completely voluntary. They also may update their Demographic Data throughout their time at the company.

Individuals have a right to withdraw their consent and opt out of sharing their non-required, voluntarily disclosed Demographic Data at any time. Where data has already been provided to a third party and an individual wishes to withdraw their consent to its use, they should notify the DGT with the notice of withdrawing consent to sharing their Demographic Data.

How Demographic Data is Used

The company limits the processing of Demographic Data to the minimum necessary and only for specific permissible purposes. The company may use and disclose Aggregated and Non-Aggregated Demographic Data for:

- Diversity, Equity, and Inclusion objectives, such as analyzing the representation of historically underrepresented groups in the talent pipeline; assessing work opportunities, staffing and pitch teams; and determining ways to increase diversity in the talent pool and improve equitable outcomes.
- Evaluating and advancing the company's Diversity, Equity, and Inclusion initiatives.
- Developing marketing and recruiting materials reflecting the company's diverse population.
- Fulfilling our obligations under applicable laws, such as government diversity reporting.
- Demonstrating the company's diverse population to current and potential customers.

Sharing Information Externally

The company may share Aggregated Demographic Data on its website and in marketing and recruiting materials.
In addition, the company may share Demographic Data

externally with:
- current clients who monitor the company's diversity efforts, otherwise benefit from the company's diversity efforts, and/or require Demographic Data for compliance with their outside counsel guidelines.
- potential clients who request Demographic Data when assessing whether to engage the company.
- service providers and other third parties who perform duties and functions on the company's behalf, such as employee survey companies or cloud service providers, which cannot use any identifying information for their own independent purposes.
- governmental agencies, or pursuant to a subpoena, court order, or decree with appropriate safeguards where feasible to protect the integrity and confidentiality of Demographic Data.

Outside of the circumstances above, the company prohibits the sharing of Individualized, Non-Aggregated Demographic Data outside of the company.

How Demographic Data is Stored
The DGT must inventory and classify, or cause to be inventoried and classified, all Demographic Data collected by the company.

All datasets containing Disaggregated, Non-Anonymized Demographic Data must be formed using only data pulled directly from a system of record (a/k/a "source of truth") as determined and designated by the company.

Any datasets, reports, or other documentation containing Disaggregated, Non-Anonymized Demographic Data must be kept in the company's document management system (DMS) if downloaded from Denodo or the system of record. Storage outside of the DMS, including on a local drive or cloud storage accounts such as Teams, SharePoint, or OneNote, is prohibited.

How Demographic Data is Secured

All Demographic Data that is collected from individuals will be kept securely. The company follows these security measures to protect Demographic Data:

- All systems housing Demographic Data must pass an information security review that is reassessed on a regular basis to ensure any new vulnerabilities are found and patched.
- All reports or datasets containing Demographic Data that are required to be aggregated or anonymized must be properly anonymized or aggregated using statistical techniques, masking, or aggregated or displayed in a non-editable format (e.g., an image in a PowerPoint).
- All datasets containing Demographic Data must be vetted by the DGT prior to sharing to ensure they cannot be combined to form a single dataset that violates a provision in this policy.
- The DGT must keep, or cause to be kept, internal logs tracking which datasets have been "checked out" and by whom, as well as any relevant revocation period.

Requests for Demographic Data and Access Restrictions

Disaggregated, Non-Anonymized Demographic Data is only available upon request and approval by the DGT. Certain company personnel, by virtue of their role(s), have standing authority to access this data. A list of these roles was developed by the Diversity, Equity, & Inclusion Team. The DGT is responsible for ensuring the appropriate permissions are set in the data platform. Data requests may be approved in whole or in part.

Any requests for Demographic Data must be submitted to the DGT via email or via Request workflow in Collibra.

Where access to Disaggregated, Non-Anonymized Demographic Data is requested:
- The Requestor must describe a legitimate business reason for requesting the data.
- The Approver must conduct a Data Privacy Impact Assessment ("DPIA") prior to authorizing access. The Approver will deny access where the DPIA shows a risk level above a certain threshold.
- If access to Demographic Data is denied, the Approver will describe the reasons for the denial to the Requestor and propose alternative methods for meeting the Requestor's goals.

The individuals receiving access to Demographic Data must:
- Acknowledge that they have read this policy.
- Keep the dataset containing Demographic Data in a private folder on the DMS. The system will detect and delete the dataset from this folder on the 31st day after download. After deletion, the Requestor must request access again.
- Handle Demographic Data in accordance with the company's Information Governance and Security Policies as found in the Company Manual.
- Only use Demographic Data for the purposes

requested. If the scope of the request changes, the requestor must inform the DGT. If the new scope is not a logical outgrowth of the original request and does not comply with acceptable uses elsewhere in this policy, the request for expanded scope will be denied.

General Restrictions
No Demographic Data may be used in automated decision-making.

No company personnel, including an approved user, may print, or cause to be printed, physical copies of Disaggregated or Non-Anonymized Demographic Data.

No company personnel, including an approved user, may disseminate electronic or physical copies of Disaggregated or Non-Anonymized Demographic Data. This prohibition includes sending the data to an approved user's personal email address.

Retention of Demographic Data
The company retains aggregated Demographic Data as long as needed for our Diversity, Equity, and Inclusion initiatives and as legally required. Individual Demographic Data is retained for seven years post-employment.

Questions or Concerns
Any questions or concerns regarding this policy or the use of Demographic Data should be directed to the company's Data Governance Team.

(To download a free copy of this template, visit happydatacompany.com/resources)

Selected Resources

Data Governance
Non-Invasive Data Governance: The Path of Least Resistance and Greatest Success by Robert S. Seiner

Data Handling
Sample Size Calculator: https://www.calculator.net/sample-size-calculator.html

Strategy Drafting
"Simple Guide To Creating A Compelling Mission and Vision Statement," Micah Logan, Forbes.
https://www.forbes.com/sites/micahlogan/2024/03/13/simple-guide-to-creating-a-compelling-mission-and-vision-statement/

"Comparison of Data Management Maturity Assessments (DMMA)," Data Strategy Professionals.
https://www.datastrategypros.com/resources/data-management-maturity-assessment-dmma

Metadata & Quality Management
ThoughtSpot Blog's guides to data modeling:
https://www.thoughtspot.com/data-trends/topics/data-model

American Society for Quality (ASQ)'s resources on root cause analysis:
https://asq.org/quality-resources/root-cause-analysis

Acknowledgments

My favorite part of writing this book was being able to collaborate with some of my favorite people. I'm truly one of the lucky ones to be surrounded by smart, generous, creative, and supportive friends and colleagues. I'd like to extend a special thanks to those who helped make this book ten times better than I could have alone: Mark Thorogood, for helping me sharpen my ideas; Anna Busch and Silina Rishmawi, for helping me make data governance joyful; and Tracy Barr, for helping me say what I mean and develop my arguments fully—long before this book was even a thought.

Index

3 Ss of Data Governance, 78
Abraham Wald, 108
AI, i, 8, 9, 11, 18, 40, 50, 59, 72, 106, 110, 111, 140, 192, 222
appeal, 126, 127, 180
Artificial Intelligence (AI). *See* AI
authority, 6, 34, 41, 42, 43, 47, 52, 66, 117, 211, 236
biases, 56, 107, 112, 114
Big Bets, 167
business agility, 16
business terms, 46, 143
business-led data management, 3, 57, 59
change management, 26, 51, 62, 67, 70, 120, 176
cherry picking, 114
chief data officer, 37, 38, 39, 40, 47
clout, 41, 47
conceptual data model, 116, 132, 133, 134
copy-paste pattern, 166, 169, 223
critical data, 49, 56, 59, 66, 77, 78, 80, 81, 83, 94, 141, 184, 211, 218, 229
culture, 12, 13, 31, 38, 58, 60, 66, 67, 152, 155, 169, 206, 223
DAMA International Data Management Body of Knolwedge
DAMA Wheel, 20, 21, 23, 24, 31, 49, 50, 56, 146, 170, 171
DAMA International Data Management Body of Knowledge, 20
data breach, 13, 14, 15, 148, 224
  Equifax, 14, 15
  Marriott, 14, 15, 17, 243
data catalog, 60, 69, 122, 123, 125, 134, 156, 157, 163, 174, 175, 180, 196, 209, 211, 212, 213, 214, 215, 217, 221, 232
data governance, 9, 11, 12, 18, 20, 23, 24, 25, 35, 37, 46, 47, 49, 50, 53, 56, 57, 58, 59, 60, 61, 62, 63, 64, 65, 66, 67, 68, 69, 70, 71, 77, 79, 89, 94, 118, 122, 123, 124, 125, 126, 127, 134, 143, 158, 167, 173, 176, 196, 209, 210, 211, 212, 214, 216, 217, 219, 220, 222, 231, 239, 243
  board, 31, 32, 43, 53, 58, 65, 66, 77, 118, 122, 125, 127, 128, 155, 196, 211, 224
  council, 43, 53, 58, 65, 66, 77, 89, 118, 122, 123, 124, 125, 126, 127, 128, 133, 134, 141, 158, 196, 211, 220, 225
  Data Governance Lifecycle, 67
  Definition, 6

Index

data lifecycle, 18
data literacy, 59, 66, 67, 114, 154, 161, 162, 171, 172, 176, 181, 182, 183, 184, 185, 191, 196, 198, 211, 225
data privacy, 13, 15, 16, 19, 23, 24, 59, 98, 101, 102, 103, 183, 222, 225
data privacy law, 13, 23, 102
   General Data Protection Regulation (GDPR), 15, 103
   Sectoral Laws, 102
   State Laws, 102
data privacy regulations. See data privacy law
data privay law
   International Laws, 103
data quality, 5, 18, 23, 49, 50, 56, 60, 66, 67, 69, 72, 82, 85, 89, 90, 93, 94, 118, 120, 123, 134, 143, 158, 173, 175, 183, 184, 185, 194, 209, 214, 220, 224, 225
Data Security, 22, 104
   availability, 104
   confidentiality, 104
   integrity, 104
data steward, 53, 58, 65, 66, 78, 81, 104, 118, 122, 124, 125, 140, 141, 142, 144, 169, 213, 220, 229
data virtualization, 135, 214, 215
domain, 52, 63, 74, 75, 77, 130, 131, 132, 134, 158, 213
ethics, 9, 66, 83, 97, 106, 114, 225, 226

fallacies, 56, 107, 114
   Hasty Generalization, 107, 108
GAPP. *See* Generally Accepted Privacy Principles
Gartner, 1, 9, 10, 61, 181
Generally Accepted Privacy Principles, 99, 100
guiding coalition, 37, 51, 52
   Credibility, 52, 53
   Expertise, 52
   Leadership, 52, 53
   Position Power, 52, 53
IKEA Effect, 116, 117
Intimidation, 164
issue management, 116, 118, 119, 120, 121, 122, 124, 137
   Communicate, 122
   Document, 120
   Resolve, 124
   Triage, 120
John P. Kotter, 51, 52
Jumping to conclusions, 164, 165
Lack of coordination, 173
Lack of enthusiasm, 174
Lack of information, 173
Lack of skill, 173
Low-Hanging Fruits, 168
master data, 49, 50, 60, 213
maturity model, 34, 71, 94
metadata, 23, 24, 49, 130, 134, 138, 140, 141, 142, 143, 145, 156, 217, 220, 221, 229
Micromanaging, 164

Money Pits, 168
Negative reaction to criticism, 164
New "X" Paradox, 38, 40
Non-Invasive Data Governance, 63
operating framework, 25, 52
  ad hoc, 30
  centralized, 25, 26, 27
  decentralized, 25, 27, 28, 130
  federated, 25, 29
  replicated, 25, 192
Operating Model. *See* operating framework
Organizational Archeology, 74, 89, 134
Over-focusing, 164
over-generalizing, 49
over-specializing, 49
panacea product, 165, 169, 170
Personal Information (PII), 98, 99, 103
persuasion, 41
  Authority, 41
  Commitment and Consistency, 41
  Liking, 41
  Reciprocity, 41
  Scarcity, 41
  Social Proof, 41
Plan, Do, Check, Act (PDCA), 90
polls, 161
random sample, 113
Robert Cialdini, 41
Robert Seiner, 63
sample size, 113
silos, 24, 32, 39, 47, 58, 61, 115, 116, 117, 118, 130, 135, 136, 169, 210, 216
source of truth. *See* system of record
spaghetti architecture, 24, 135, 136
surveys, 161
system of record, 73, 77, 78, 79, 80, 82, 89, 90, 142, 144, 206, 207, 214, 220, 221, 234, 235
taxonomy, 134
technology-led governance, 57
The Quick Wins Paradox, 164
word-of-mouth, 160
zombie projects, 170

Notes

Chapter One: I Dream of Data

1 We connect data management with data governance here because data governance guides all other data management functions.
2 Earley, Susan. 2017. DAMA-DMBOK : Data Management Body of Knowledge. 2nd ed. Basket Ridge, New Jersey: Technics Publications, pp. 16–17.
3 Covey, Stephen. 1989. 7 Habits of Highly Effective People. Simon & Schuster.
4 Judah, Saul, and Andrew White. 2020. Review of The State of Data and Analytics Governance Is Worse than You Think. Gartner, June. https://www.gartner.com/document-reader/document/3986529.
5 Krebs, Brian. 2017. Review of Equifax Breach Response Turns Dumpster Fire. Krebs on Security. September 8, 2017. krebsonsecurity.com/2017/09/equifax-breach-response-turns-dumpster-fire/.
6 EPIC.org. 2021. "EPIC - Equifax Data Breach." Archive.epic.org. 2021. https://archive.epic.org/privacy/data-breach/equifax/.
7 Monica, Paul R. La. 2017. "Equifax Shares Plunge Again -- 35% in Past Week." CNNMoney. September 14, 2017. https://money.cnn.com/2017/09/14/investing/equifax-stock/index.html.
8 FTC. 2019. "Equifax to Pay $575 Million as Part of Settlement with FTC, CFPB, and States Related to 2017 Data Breach." Federal Trade Commission. July 22, 2019. https://www.ftc.gov/news-events/news/press-releases/2019/07/equifax-pay-575-million-part-settlement-ftc-cfpb-states-related-2017-data-breach.
9 Husain, Osman. 2023. Review of 10 Privacy Breach Examples: Lessons Learned & How to Prevent Them. Www.enzuzo.com (blog). June 23, 2023. www.enzuzo.com/blog/privacy-breach-examples.
10 Marriott International. 2023 Annual Report. 2023.
11 Brown, Eileen. 2020. "One in Four Americans Won't Do Business with Data-Breached Companies." ZDNet. February 28, 2020.

https://www.zdnet.com/article/one-in-four-americans-wont-do-business-with-data-breached-companies/.

12   UNCTAD. 2021. "Data Protection and Privacy Legislation Worldwide | UNCTAD." Unctad.org. December 14, 2021. https://unctad.org/page/data-protection-and-privacy-legislation-worldwide.

13   Prybylski, Hank. n.d. "Two Years into the Pandemic, Digital Transformation Is Moving Forward: Here's How." Forbes. https://www.forbes.com/sites/hankprybylski/2022/05/04/two-years-into-the-pandemic-digital-transformation-is-moving-forward-heres-how/.

14   Blog, Data & Policy. 2023. "Interwoven Realms: Data Governance as the Bedrock for AI Governance." Data & Policy Blog. November 20, 2023. https://medium.com/data-policy/interwoven-realms-data-governance-as-the-bedrock-for-ai-governance-ffd56a6a4543.

[15]   Earley, Susan. 2017. DAMA-DMBOK : Data Management Body of Knowledge. 2nd ed. Basket Ridge, New Jersey: Technics Publications.

[16]   The DAMA-DMBOK refers to a decentralized approach as "replicated."

Chapter Two: The Data Bunch

17   Rakhin V. 2022. "15 New C-Suite Titles: Hype or Here to Stay? - SmartKarrot Blog." SmartKarrot L Customer Success Software. April 12, 2022. https://www.smartkarrot.com/resources/blog/new-c-suite-titles/.

18 Team, RC. 2020. "The 10 Strangest Job Titles Used by Real Companies." ResumeCoach. April 3, 2020. https://www.resumecoach.com/10-strangest-job-titles-used-by-real-companies/.

19 Cialdini, Robert B. Influence: The Psychology of Persuasion. 1984.

20 "The Blind Men and the Elephant." n.d. Www.peacecorps.gov. https://www.peacecorps.gov/educators/resources/blind-men-and-elephant/story-blind-men-and-elephant/.

21 Earley, Susan. 2017. DAMA-DMBOK : Data Management Body of Knowledge. 2nd ed. Basket Ridge, New Jersey: Technics Publications, pp. 554.

22 Earley, Susan. 2017. DAMA-DMBOK : Data Management Body of

Knowledge. 2nd ed. Basket Ridge, New Jersey: Technics Publications, pp. 551-52.

Chapter Three: Happy Data

23 Our body of work was informed by activities described in the DAMA-DMBOK, Gartner research, and our own experience. We encourage you to make liberal use of these resources to define the broad activities of your Data Governance program. The implementation and specific projects are what will make your program unique to your organization.

24 Earley, Susan. 2017. DAMA-DMBOK : Data Management Body of Knowledge. 2nd ed. Basket Ridge, New Jersey: Technics Publications, pp. 428–43.

25 Root cause analyses are beyond the scope of this book, but we started with a simple fishbone diagram and the "5 whys" to great effect.

26 "The Right to Privacy — Louis D. Brandeis School of Law Library." n.d. Louisville.edu. https://louisville.edu/law/library/special-collections/the-louis-d.-brandeis-collection/the-right-to-privacy.

27 Review of Historical Background on Fourth Amendment. n.d. Constitution Annotated. Library of Congress. https://constitution.congress.gov/browse/essay/amdt4-2/ALDE_00013706/.

28 While foundational, these rights are limited. For example, one is free to marry a person of any color or sex. But, in the US, it is not legal to marry more than one person at a time.

29 Purdue University. n.d. "Logical Fallacies." Purdue Writing Lab. Purdue University. https://owl.purdue.edu/owl/general_writing/academic_writing/logic_in_argumentative_writing/fallacies.html.

30 Dobbert, Chris. 2020. "The Missing Bullet Holes and Abraham Wald." Medium. September 22, 2020. https://medium.com/@christian.dobbert/the-missing-bullet-holes-and-abraham-wald-25e68d7a870f.

31 "Statistical Fallacies and How to Avoid Them." n.d. Geckoboard. https://www.geckoboard.com/best-practice/statistical-fallacies/.

32 "Associates degrees awarded in Mathematics and statistics correlates

with Google searches for 'dollar store near me' (r=0.991)." 2024 Tylervigen.com. 2024. https://tylervigen.com/spurious/correlation/1783_associates-degrees-awarded-in-mathematics-and-statistics_correlates-with_google-searches-for-dollar-store-near-me.

33 Review of Entry Statistician Salary in the United States. n.d. Salary.com. https://www.salary.com/research/salary/alternate/entry-statistician-salary.

34 "Associates degrees awarded in Mathematics and statistics correlates with Google searches for 'dollar store near me' (r=0.991)." 2024 Tylervigen.com. 2024.

Chapter Four: Gilligan's Data

35 "Quote Origin: A Camel Is a Horse That Was Designed by a Committee – Quote Investigator®." 2023. Quoteinvestigator.com. September 22, 2023. https://quoteinvestigator.com/2023/09/22/horse-camel/.

36 Earley, Susan. 2017. DAMA-DMBOK : Data Management Body of Knowledge. 2nd ed. Basket Ridge, New Jersey: Technics Publications, pp. 84.

Chapter Five: Data Knows Best

37 Huebbe, Patricia, and Gerald Rimbach. 2020. "Historical Reflection of Food Processing and the Role of Legumes as Part of a Healthy Balanced Diet." Foods 9 (8): 1056. https://doi.org/10.3390/foods9081056.

38 Gershon, Livia. 2022. "Where Do Nutrition Labels Come From?" JSTOR Daily. October 23, 2022. https://daily.jstor.org/where-do-nutrition-labels-come-from/.

39 We tried to find the original source for this framework but were unsuccessful. If an eagle-eyed reader out there is reading this endnote and knows the origin, please let us know.

40 Buren, Mark E. Van, and Todd Safferstone. 2009. "The Quick Wins Paradox." Harvard Business Review. January 1, 2009. https://hbr.org/2009/01/the-quick-wins-paradox.

Chapter Six: Data, She Wrote

41 Rulf, Dana. n.d. "This Is Why Our Brain Loves Pictures | International Forum of Visual Practitioners." Ifvp.org. https://ifvp.org/content/why-our-brain-loves-pictures.

42 The media education centre. n.d. "Using Images Effectively in Media." https://oit.williams.edu/files/2010/02/using-images-effectively.pdf.

43 K-means clustering is a type of algorithm that groups a collection of data points together based on shared characteristics.

44 A/B testing is a method of comparing two versions of something to see which performs better.

45 Lorincz, Nikolett. 2024. "What Is a Good CTR? Average Click-through Rate for Google Ads, Facebook Ads & Email Campaigns." OptiMonk - Popups, Supercharged. February 27, 2024. https://www.optimonk.com/what-is-a-good-ctr/#:~:text=Let.

www.ingramcontent.com/pod-product-compliance
Lightning Source LLC
Chambersburg PA
CBHW030014040426
42337CB00012BA/781